REVEALED *The Archetypes*

As Apostle of Christian Families Against Destructive Decisions (CFADD), It is my honor to recommend this thought-provoking book, *Revealed: The Archetypes of American Politics—'Overlords,' 'House Negroes,' and 'Field Negroes!'* I enthusiastically recommend this book for all readers who are committed to understanding the profound dynamics of American society, partic`ularly as they pertain to the relationships between power, freedom, and individual responsibility. This book powerfully exposes the ideological strongholds that have kept so many in bondage—whether they realize it or not—and provides readers with a roadmap to personal liberation and the restoration of our God-given rights.

The author's deep exploration into the archetypes of American politics is both eye-opening and crucial to understanding the spiritual, social, and political challenges we face today. His analysis is grounded in historical realities yet speaks directly to our current political landscape, making the connections necessary for us to see how our personal freedoms are continuously being threatened by forces that seek to divide and conquer.

What makes this book especially vital is its call to action. It challenges readers not to passively accept the cultural and political systems that enslave us but instead to rise up, break free from these bonds, and reclaim the principles of freedom, morality, and righteousness that our ancestors fought to secure.

For pastors, educators, and leaders—this book will serve as a powerful tool to guide your congregation or community towards truth and liberation. For individuals, it will embolden you to live out your calling as a free child of God, exercising wisdom and discernment in every area of life. I cannot recommend this work enough as it aligns perfectly with our mission at CFADD: to build strong families and nations by a biblical worldview. ~ **Apostle Tommy E. Quick, Founder, CFADD (cfadd.org)**

My wife Beverly and I met Dr. Kevin McGary about a year ago at a gathering of prominent Black leaders given by The Douglas Leadership Institute. Even then he stood out as an exquisite piece of jewelry in a field of diamonds. In this, his new book he continues that tradition. The title, though politically incorrect, is an intentional action to bolster you, the reader from your perch of peaceful cultural satisfaction to one of cultural inquiry.

In this book, Dr. McGary has taken current iconic cultural talking points and exposed them to proven imperial truths to reveal the damage they've caused not only in the Black Community but the nation as well. Critical thinking is the mantra of this book. If you are looking for a palatable reading experience to confirm your having accepted current cultural trends you will walk away with a new perspective. Either you will be honest enough to recognize your current position and make changes or you will dismiss his presentation with malice. There is only room for either this guy has given the reader room for thought or the price of action on the part of the reader is too high. Kudos Dr. McGary for a job well done… an "OUTSTANDING READ!" ~ **Rodney/Beverly Mayberry**, **African American Council**

Mr. McGary has produced another mind-blowing book that destroys logic lines built on fallacy, hyperbole, and mass misinformation! Every chapter produces paradigm-shifting points that make the status quo impossible for intellectual and spiritual connoisseurs of Truth! ~ **Dr. Howard Hatcher**, **Author of Trump 45 & The Black Man Parallel**

While many shy away from sensitive and challenging topics to avoid discomfort or division, Kevin McGary tackles them head-on with boldness, dismantling entrenched mindsets and ideologies. Revealed! challenges long-held assumptions about political allegiance within the African American community, offering a fresh perspective rooted in truth, history, and faith. McGary's insights are both timely and transformative, making this a must-read for those seeking a deeper understanding of the forces shaping our society. **~ Pastor Lucas Miles, Sr. Director of TPUSA Faith and Author of Woke Jesus**

REVEALED: THE ARCHETYPES OF AMERICAN POLITICS...

'Overlords,' 'House Negroes,' and 'Field Negroes!' Which One Are You?

DR. MACK

RATIONAL FREE PRESS
Boise • Silicon Valley • Toronto

Dr. Bell,
Read and consider, "Which one are you?"
Enjoy!! :)
Love, Dr. Mack,

ISBN: 978-1-7382891-3-4 (paperback)

Table of Contents

Author's note

Understanding history through the lens of archetypes and the underlying motivations of those who resisted bondage and escaped to freedom is essential.

Though this book may at first seem a deep dive into the inner workings of personal motives, it is, at its heart, a study of history. By examining the struggles and triumphs of American heroes who broke free from the chains of tyranny, oppression, and slavery, we glimpse not only their unyielding pursuit of freedom but the timeless truths they impart to us. Figures such as Frederick Douglass, Harriet Tubman, and Sojourner Truth do more than inspire; they reveal to us the fierce vigilance required to win—and more importantly, to preserve—liberty.

Their lives are a testament to the resilience of the human spirit and their stories, if we heed them, become a blueprint for our own defense of freedom. As we face growing threats to our liberties today, we must turn to these lessons with renewed attention. For it is by understanding both the archetypes they represent and the inner forces that drove them that we will learn what it means to move forward— toward Freedom.

Introduction

Over the past few decades, the American political environment has grown increasingly polarized, tribal, and antagonistic, making even casual discussions about politics fraught with danger. This escalation in hostility is not a natural phenomenon, but rather a symptom of deeper, systemic dysfunction. To understand the forces driving this hostility, we must examine three entrenched psychological frameworks, or "pathologies," that have come to dominate the political landscape. These frameworks represent deviations from normal behavior and have transformed into powerful, calculated tools of control.

Historical operations like Project Paperclip and the Negro Project, coupled with mass propaganda efforts enabled by the Smith-Mundt Act, have actively contributed to the entrenchment of political pathologies. After reading, you will more fully grasp how these pervasive schemes are being used as purposeful tools to control Americans, and limit freedom.

Figures like Malcolm X, who had a keen understanding of the psychological and social mechanisms underpinning phenomena driving divisions and distrust illustrated how specific archetypes persist in American society. Specifically, he identified three central archetypes and associated pathologies: the *House Negro*, the *Field Negro*, and the *Overlord*. Each represents a distinct mentality that impacts political and social dynamics in ways that perpetuate division and control.

By unpacking these archetypes and understanding the historical underpinnings and manipulation behind them, we can better grasp the root causes of our current plight of political dysfunction in the American political landscape.

Malcolm X used the term negro liberally. For perspective, it is important to clarify that the term "negro" in this book is not intended as a pejorative. It is not meant to be associated with derogatory slang or viewed through the lens of race, skin color, or ethnicity. The term "negro" here is used in conjunction with "house" or "field" to signify a condition of the soul and psyche that drives actions and intentions. These terms are used to help better observe and distinguish as we unveil the pervasive mindsets of the "House Negro," the "Field Negro," and the "Overlord," social constructs that Malcolm X famously characterized and popularized in 1963.

The book title may initially seem harsh or hyperbolic to some due to the historical association of the word "negro" with race, particularly African Americans. However, in this context, "negro" strictly represents a mindset or archetype—a way of thinking and behaving that transcends race or ethnicity. It is used to describe overarching mindsets that permeate the American political landscape.

In this book, we will delve into these mindsets, revealing how they shape our political ideas, interactions, and societal structures. Understanding these mindsets as archetypes (overarching themes) will not only provide clarity but also empower you to navigate the complexities of contemporary American politics without having to equivocate or downplay the significance of the terms to appease sophomoric demands for political correctness.

From the title of this book, the audacious question, "Which one are you?", implies that you inevitably fit into one of these categories. It's not a typo. Every American voter, consciously or not, falls entirely into one of these archetypes (house negro, field negro, or overlord). These archetypes are not just theoretical constructs, but they are deeply embedded in the American political landscape. No one is an outside observer of these pervasive mindsets. No ethnicity is exempt. As every American voter fits into one of these archetypes, this book is designed to confirm how each voter possesses the underlying mindset and actions that place them within these categories.

This book aims to use historical writings and speeches about life on the plantation as a backdrop to help guide readers toward identifying their psychological archetype and determining which category they belong to. It's not meant to comfort or delude; it's designed to orient readers to prevailing psyches driving the American political landscape. By recognizing and embracing one's true self (and respective orientations), readers will be able to mitigate self-deception and personal delusions about how and why one participates in American politics. Delusion can erode integrity, becoming a cancer to the soul. Thus, this book is dedicated to helping readers achieve clarity, honesty, and healing through self-awareness.

Every American over the age of 18, the legal voting age, fits into one of the archetypal mindsets discussed in this book. Therefore, the distinctions used are undeniable realities and inescapable (ubiquitous), so it is essential to recognize which category each individual belongs to. While these mindsets can influence all domains of life—such as education, work, finance, media, entertainment, spirituality, and community—examining the house negro, field negro, and overlord archetypes through the lens of American politics offers a clearer understanding of the actions and behaviors that are most identifiable and prevalent in our current times. The urgency of this self-discovery cannot be overstated.

Whether you react to American politics with uncontrollable anger, visceral hatred, and unhinged outbursts or through principles, logic, reason, morals, and a desire for peace, there is a definitive category you belong to.

The challenge for each reader is to discern: "Which one are you?"

One

Unmasking And Exposing the Pathology of The House Negro

An excerpt from Malcolm X's speech "Message to the Grassroots" delivered in 1963:

"There was two kinds of slaves. There was the house negro and the field negro. The house negroes—they lived in the house with master, they dressed pretty good, they ate good 'cause they ate his food—what he left. They lived in the attic or the basement, but still they lived near the master; and they loved the master more than the master loved himself. They would give their life to save the master's house—quicker than the master would. The house negro, if the master said, 'We got a good house here,' the house negro would say, 'Yeah, we got a good house here.' Whenever the

*master said 'we,' he said 'we.' That's how you can tell
a house negro."*[1]

Not long ago, Americans could hold differing opinions
about politics and "respectfully disagree" without resort-
ing to insults and pejoratives. Those days are long gone. Today,
dissenting voices, especially those rejecting Leftist, Marxist, or
Progressive ideologies, are often deemed irredeemably de-
plorable and "racist." Why has American political discourse
degraded to this level? Why has political dialogue become
so abusive and relentless? The pathology of the house negro
mindset explains it all.

It is way past time the "House Negro," a term popularized
by Malcolm X, is examined and more thoroughly understood.
Understanding the house negro as a syndrome distinct from
race or ethnicity is crucial. Based on the level of cultural pressure and intensity applied to get others to conform, I believe
the most pervasive mindset dominating the American political
landscape today is that of the house negro. It may seem ironic,
but since any race, ethnicity, skin color, or class can embody
this mindset, white Americans seemingly make up the majority
of those under the spell of house negro syndrome.

With Progressives using tactics and schemes leveraging
"cancel culture" and castigation via unbridled vitriol to demand conformity to Leftist progressivism, we can observe the

---

[1] Transcribed speech via Columbia Univ., https://ccnmtl.columbia.edu/projects/
mmt/mxp/speeches/mxa17.html

pathology of the house negro.[2] Since statistics show the overwhelming majority of Leftist Progressives are white, it is easy to surmise whites (by majority) make up the landscape of those who embody the mindset of house negroes. No doubt, many may attempt to reject this notion. Still, due to its transcendent yet pervasive nature, coupled with its veiled subtleties, it is often unrecognizable. Many have been so thoroughly brainwashed into the pathology of the house negro that they lack the capacity to see the embrace of this insidious underpinning. The house negro mindset has gained an unshakable stronghold rooted in their souls, producing its tell-tale outcomes. It is past time for this corrosive pathology to be thoroughly examined and unveiled.

EMERGENCE OF HOUSE NEGRO SYNDROME

During America's centuries of slavery, distinct mindsets and convoluted interactions emerged among those in bondage. In his 1963 speech, Malcolm X identified new social constructs that provide insight into distinct mindsets driving the actions, intentions, and interactions of enslaved people. Interestingly, while everyone on the plantation was enslaved (the only truly free individual was the plantation overlord), subcategories and associated actions emerged, exacerbating the interpersonal dynamics of slavery and further complicating their shared suffering and plight.

---

[2]   Very liberal, highly educated and majority White, https://www.pewresearch.org/politics/2021/11/09/progressive-left/

As African American slaves endured inhuman treatment and grotesque abuse from overlords, common sense might suggest that all slaves, regardless of their station, would desire to overthrow their oppressors and escape to freedom. But this was not the case. The actions and intentions of the house negro exacerbated the plight of fellow slaves and increased the difficulty of escaping to freedom. They protected the interests of overlords at all costs, thoroughly rejecting the dire needs and severe situations of fellow slaves. What causes those experiencing enslavement together to divide themselves in order to curry favor with their captors? What motivated the house negroes? One word: recompense. They were paid to do so.

Understanding this historical context helps us see how these dynamics continue to play out in modern American political discourse, where the house negro mindset becomes pervasive and vastly contributes to the degradation of civil dialogue and the perpetuation of division and hostility.

UNPACKING THE PATHOLOGY OF HOUSE NEGROES

Malcolm neatly characterized it: The house negro was loyal (to a fault) to his "master" (overlord). He enjoyed significantly better living conditions and often identified more with the master's interests than with those of fellow enslaved people in the fields. These accommodations were his form of payment for obedience and surrender to the "slave state." Being compensated in various ways while enjoying close proximity and association with the power structure of the overlord was seductive and compelling. That comfort clouded the house negroes view and undermined his empathy concerning the trauma and pain of fellow slaves, and that was what made the house negro dangerous.

THE ROLE AND ACTIONS OF HOUSE NEGROES

Often, it was house negroes who would snitch on those who were scheming to escape the plantation. Snitching was so widespread that it was understood that if other slaves escaped, perhaps the house negro had not done his "job." The house negro was supposed to be the "eyes and ears" of the plantation owner, and therefore, he was committed to preventing any other slaves from escaping. As long as there was a healthy crop of slaves, the house negro was en-sured to have power and authority over them. He was mo-tivated to keep slaves on the plantation. As long as he did, he would further ingratiate himself to the "all-powerful" overlord. House negroes readily prioritized alignment with any of their masters' oppressive systems for personal gain or relative comfort. The broader interests of other slaves were ignored in deference to personal gain through various forms of recompense (some form of compensation) from the overlord. That said, house negroes (then and now) rep-resent the epitome of an archetype that is self-serving and loathsome.

UNDERLYING SOCIOPATHOLOGY OF HOUSE NEGROES

In his book "The Slave Community: Plantation Life in the Antebellum South,"[3] author John W. Blassingame describes the house negro as follows: "The house servant, by virtue of his proximity to the master and his family, often became a tragic figure, caught between two worlds—privileged in some respects, yet despised by both the master and the field hands." This quote encapsulates the duality and inner conflict (sociopathology) experienced by house slaves, who were often seen as both favored and mistrusted, leading to a precarious existence on the plantation.

With various forms of recompense, including the best clothes (house negroes would be first to receive hand-me-downs from their master), choice table scraps (they would have first dibs on food scraps from the master's table), being able to sleep in the plantation house (usually attic or basement, but better than the field), and frequent encounters and close associations with the master/overlord, the house negro was seemingly under a spell. It presented as a psychosis that prompted delusions of grandeur. In the end, the house negro was still a slave to the master, but the delusions made him feel "better," different and "elite."

Delusions precipitated by the house negro mentality involved a deep-seated loyalty to the master; on balance, this relationship appears irrational, however. The master/overlord

---

[3] Blassingame, John W. *The Slave Community: Plantation Life in the Antebellum South*. New York: Oxford University Press, 1972

was abusive and meted out generous amounts of tyranny to the enslaved, their respective families, and their communities. But the house negro often rationalized and justified oppressively abusive behaviors and systems in order to maintain personal benefit. This mindset is characterized by a belief that their well-being is tied to the maintenance of the master/overlord status quo (maintain the master-slave dichotomy), even if the status quo undermines a commitment to personal dignity.

In John W. Blassingame's "The Slave Community: Plantation Life in the Antebellum South," he provides insight into the duplicitous mindset of house negroes: "While many house servants developed a sense of superiority over the field hands, they were often the objects of the master's sexual exploitation and, thus, in a more precarious position than the field hands." Despite being vulnerable to rape, sexual exploitation, and abuse, house negroes often found ways to excuse their vulnerabilities to maintain a close connection with the power of the plantation overlord. This quote highlights the complex and contradictory experiences of house negroes, who, despite certain privileges, remained deeply vulnerable to exploitation and abuse.

As it was experienced on the plantation, the house negro syndrome provided a perfect example of a psychosis called "betrayal blindness."

THE HOUSE NEGRO'S PSYCHOSIS OF BETRAYAL BLINDNESS

Betrayal blindness refers to a psychological phenomenon where individuals remain unaware of, or purposely choose to ignore, instances of betrayal, abuse, or exploitation perpetrated by a person or system they are dependent upon or loyal to.[4] In the context of the house negro, betrayal blindness is evident when an individual, despite recognizing the oppressive nature and injustices of the overlord, chooses to overlook or rationalize these betrayals to maintain their perceived security, privileges, or status with the overlord. Based on historical writings and associated actions of house negroes, betrayal blindness seems to have been necessarily a continual state of personal deception; this is a prescribed level of what can be deemed "delusional pathology."

Despite witnessing the brutality and harsh treatment meted out to field slaves, house negroes rationalized their own relatively better treatment as indicative of the master's benevolence. This rationalization led them to remain loyal to the master, even to the extent of snitching on fellow slaves who planned rebellions or escapes, thereby ensuring the perpetuation of the cycle of oppression.

A house negro suffering from acute betrayal blindness would idly stand by as the master/overlord abuses or assaults his wife and or children. He is human and not blind, so he would certainly recognize the abuse or assault as abusive but would rationalize the horror of the event(s) by telling himself that the overlord must have a reason and his brutality is needed to send a message for the demand of complete obedience.

---

[4] Betrayal Blindness, Psychology Today- https://www.psychologytoday.com/us/blog/brothers-sisters-strangers/202312/betrayal-blindness-not-seeing-whats-obvious

House negroes wholly bought into a mindset that prioritizes their (selfish) personal benefits over logical, moral, and righteous thinking that would have them stridently pursue just treatment for all. They sought to maintain their privileged position by aligning with the oppressive inclinations of the overlord, even if it meant betraying and undermining their peers. To be fair, fear and the corrosive nature of the demands of the overlord also played into the house negroes desire for self-preservation. He knew that to go against the wishes of the overlord would risk losing his elevated position amongst the slaves and would incur the wrath of the master at the same rate (or even more so) than the overall slave community, including the field negroes.

For reasons of cowardice, desperation, or just self-preservation to advance personal ambition, betrayal blindness was readily embraced by the house negro. The only expectation one could have for those stricken by the house negro mindset is that once rooted, it will always conform to the dictates of the overlord. Even if a house negro found a way to escape this tyrannically abusive relationship temporarily, he would often come back to the master. Outside observers would not be able to understand this, but this confirms a pathology that is likened to what we call Stockholm Syndrome.

THE HOUSE NEGROES CONNECTION TO STOCKHOLM SYNDROME

Stockholm Syndrome is a sociopathological disorder that is confirmed by individuals adopting positive feelings towards those who harm, abuse, and misuse them. When captives fall victim to the syndrome, overlords, oppressors, and/or captors are allowed to continue meting out abusive tactics upon victims without consequences.[5] Often, victims captivated and entrapped by Stockholm Syndrome embrace rationalizing and defending actions of the overlord (or oppressor) as a survival mechanism.

STOCKHOLM SYNDROME EXPLAINED AND ILLUSTRATED

Stockholm Syndrome is a psychosis whereby hostages (or slaves) actually develop a bond with their captors. A glaring example of Stockholm Syndrome can be observed in the biblical narrative of the Israelites who, despite their harsh enslavement in Egypt, expressed a desire to return to their life of abusive slavery and bondage after being freed. (Numbers 14:1-4) This narrative provides profound insights into the complexities of human psychology under prolonged oppression and the ways in which the oppressed can develop attachments to their oppressors.

The Israelites endured centuries of brutal slavery under the Egyptians and were subjected to harsh labor, cruel punishments, and a life devoid of freedom. Yet, when Moses led them out of Egypt towards the Promised Land, the journey was fraught with uncertainty. They faced many hardships of the desert, and some of the Israelites expressed a longing to return to the familiar, albeit oppressive, conditions of their Egyptian slavery.

---

[5] Stockholm Syndrome- https://www.britannica.com/science/Stockholm-syndrome

The Israelites' desire to return to Egypt can be viewed through the lens of Stockholm Syndrome, where prolonged captivity and harsh treatment lead individuals to develop emotional bonds with their captors. This bond often stems from a survival instinct, where identifying with the captor and adhering to their rules becomes a strategy to avoid harm.

In the Book of Numbers, which is part of the Old Testament in the Bible, the Israelites' desire to return to Egypt is poignantly illustrated:

"We remember the fish we ate in Egypt at no cost—also the cucumbers, melons, leeks, onions, and garlic. But now we have lost our appetite; we never see anything but this manna!" (Numbers 11:5-6, NIV). This lamentation highlights how the Israelites selectively remembered the few comforts of their enslavement while overlooking the severe brutality they endured. The narrative of the Israelites longing to return to Egyptian slavery serves as a powerful example of Stockholm Syndrome. It underscores how prolonged oppression can warp perceptions and create emotional bonds with oppressors. Understanding this psychological phenomenon sheds light on the complexities of human behavior under extreme duress and the profound impact of prolonged captivity on the human psyche.

The 'house negro archetype' and mindset arise from the desperate need for self-preservation and the insatiable need to remain viable to the overlord/master. Both are unhealthy as they keep the slave inextricably entangled in irrationally abusive structures. While betrayal blindness and Stockholm Syndrome appear expedient (especially to the need for self-preservation), they ultimately undermine the personal health, security, and dignity of the individual and the community. With the pressures of these powerful pathologies, many people in these situations are compelled just blindly to follow the dictates of oppression and control. A passive group of "followers" (people who "get on the bandwagon") forms around the power centers, and those followers fall into the category of house negro.

THE BANDWAGON EFFECT: HOW AND WHY HOUSE NEGROES FOLLOW

The "bandwagon effect" is a psychological phenomenon in which people are inclined to do something just because other people are doing it (irrespective of their core values and beliefs).[6] The bandwagon effect is another subset of psychosis intertwined with the house negro syndrome. It can intersect in ways that reinforce and amplify a cycle of conformity and complicity within oppressive systems.

The bandwagon effect invites an aggregation of "followers" (as opposed to "leaders" or those possessing independent thought). The "follower" individuals adopt behaviors, attitudes, or beliefs simply because they perceive that many others are doing the same. It's a form of social influence where people conform to the majority opinion or trend, often out of a desire to belong or avoid conflict. This is part of the pathology of the house negro syndrome.

---

[6]   What is The Bandwagon Effect? Why People Follow The Crowd, June 29, 2023 https://www.investopedia.com/terms/b/bandwagon-effect.asp

When the bandwagon effect takes hold among those with "house negro syndrome," it exacerbates the tendency to conform to the oppressive overlord/master. If a significant number of house slaves or those in similar positions start to align with the enslaver's interests—perhaps due to perceived benefits like better treatment or privileges—others are compelled to follow suit, even if it means betraying their community or values. The desire to belong to this "in-group" of favored slaves can lead to the widespread adoption of attitudes that support the existing power structure, further solidifying the divide between house and field slaves.

This social dynamic weakens the oppressed people's resistance to oppression. Those affected by the bandwagon effect are discouraged from rebellion or solidarity with more defiant individuals (like those with the field negro mindset). Instead of challenging the system, the spread of house negro syndrome through the bandwagon effect leads to a more entrenched, self-perpetuating cycle of subservience and complicity.

LIFE DYNAMICS ON THE PLANTATION

On the plantation, house negroes were notorious for violating their own conscience. They constantly deluded themselves into thinking that they were promoting the "greater good" for the plantation. This way of thinking was a performative contradiction, as their actions were almost always contrary to their own sense of morality, faith, and principled convictions. House negroes were loyal to their masters to a fault and likewise disloyal to their fellow slaves in ways that cost those slaves dearly.

As stated, house negroes were conditioned to be more loyal to their master/overlord than to their own family, fellow slaves, and their faith. It is said house negroes would help their master write speeches and sermons trumpeting the merit and necessity of slavery at the expense of their own faith commitment and the peril of their fellow slaves. They thus lived in a perpetual state of cognitive dissonance that seemingly became a sociopathology that would delude the mind and consume the soul.

Overwhelmed with feelings of threat, fear, and dependence, house negroes lived a lie (the lie that they were actually working for the greater good) and took actions that readily betrayed personal convictions. They learned to live and embrace a grand falsehood, and in playing their "role," they lost their sense of identity. The inner turmoil created by a pathology that forces living a lie, embracing the actions of a brutal master, and tacitly encouraging the abuse of fellow slaves led house negroes to become vengeful and bitter.

A lack of integrity and dignity fostered significant pathological torment to the psyche of house negroes. They seemed to have assuaged the inner turmoil by doubling down on the treatment of other slaves, as their communication and actions were mostly vengeful and wrought with bitterness. Those slaves working in the fields endured great stress and turmoil.

In Frederick Douglass's "Narrative of the Life of Frederick Douglass, an American Slave,"[7] he captures the tension be-

---

[7]   Douglass, Frederick. *Narrative of the Life of Frederick Douglass, an American Slave*. Boston: Anti-Slavery Office, 1845

tween house and field slaves: "The slaves selected to go to the Great House Farm, for the monthly allowance for themselves and their fellow slaves, were peculiarly enthusiastic. While on their way, they would make the dense old woods, for miles around, reverberate with their wild songs, revealing at once the highest joy and the deepest sadness. They seemed to realize the impossibility of uttering in words their thoughts and feelings." This quote reflects some of the complex emotions of slaves (house negroes) chosen to perform tasks closer to the master's (overlord) household. Although these slaves were granted certain privileges, their joy was tinged with deep sadness, symbolizing the underlying tensions and the harsh reality of their shared abuse and oppression along with field negroes.

Unlike the relative comforts of the house negro, the field negro suffered a "double whammy." They suffered endless abuse from plantation overlords and also countless ways of maltreatment at the hands of house negroes. Plantation overlords demanded hard work and obedience, and house negroes kept a watchful eye on them to ensure they complied. While overlords used their "iron fist" in demanding compliance from every slave on the plantation, house negroes also used harsh tactics in demanding compliance from fellow slaves working in the fields. Along with the overlord, house negroes used threats, coercion, and intimidation. With the demands of their position (house negro), no doubt, gratuitous name-calling and shaming were frequently used to maximize conformity in keeping field slaves working hard while preventing escape from the plantation.

The dynamic of interactions on the plantation was that of overlords compelling torment, house negroes encouraging and supporting overlords, and field negroes always looking for a way to escape their plight. For the field negro, pain, abuse, and torment under the thumb of another was not an acceptable plight, and the need for escape became paramount.

DECODING THE MODERN PSYCHE OF THE HOUSE NEGRO

When discussing the concept of the house negro, an important question arises, prompting us to engage in self-reflection for clarity. Since the distinctions between the field negro and the "overlord" have not yet been fully explored and explained, it may be premature to definitively determine which of these pervasive psyches you embody.

Imagine asking, "Are you a house negro?" Most Americans would likely say no. However, I believe the reality of today's political landscape suggests otherwise. I assert that many Americans, seemingly the majority, align with the mindset of the house negro—not to cast aspersions on the electorate, but based on undeniable patterns that have emerged over the past several decades, this seems very much the case.

American culture has been on a downward trajectory for years. This is an indisputable fact. Marxism, encompassing both socialism and communism, has gained significant popularity and acceptance, while American patriotism, traditions, and capitalism have waned. Why is this? When we try to help others reignite the core principles that have made America a beacon of hope, freedom, and success, coupled with the importance of preserving morality and faith, our efforts are often met with shrill derision. Faced with such aggressive resistance, most Americans choose to acquiesce and cower in order to "keep the peace." People giving in to perceived group thinking is the bandwagon effect or the Stockholm Syndrome and gives rise to widespread betrayal blindness

The psyche of the house negro infiltrates the American political landscape in countless ways. One clear example is the aggressive tactics of "ethno-narcissism." This tactic labels any viewpoints supporting American traditions or the reinvigoration of its exceptional history as inherently racist, implying that all of American history and its traditions are rooted in racism. By deliberately stoking racial divisions and using grotesque racial tropes—such as accusations of racism, white supremacy, and white nationalism—those employing this tactic aim to shame, guilt, blame, and threaten anyone who dares to stand up for American traditions, morality, faith, and merit. Again, why has political discourse in America become so toxic and corrosive? The answer lies in the widespread influence of the house negro pathology.

The mindset and pathology of the house negro should not be underestimated. This behavior prioritizes the agendas of the overlord over established principles and morals. For example, despite Dr. Martin Luther King Jr.'s powerful call for Americans to judge each other based on character rather than skin color, many people are now embracing divisive ideologies like Critical Race Theory (CRT) and Diversity, Equity, and

Inclusion (DEI). These ideologies reintroduce the focus on skin color as a primary determinant in social interactions, and dissenting voices are silenced, leading to their acceptance and entrenchment in society.

In the past, the Bill of Rights, especially the 1st and 2nd Amendments, was considered sacred and non-negotiable. However, there is now a growing sentiment that free speech should be restricted, which goes against the principle of free expression.[8] Additionally, a majority of Americans now support stricter gun control laws, reflecting a significant shift in public opinion on the Second Amendment.[9] The troubling reality is that the demands of those in power now take precedence over the guiding principles of the nation. The behavior akin to the house negro only serves to accelerate and entrench these mandates, leading America away from reasoned political discourse and undermining its foundational values.

The days of "reasoning together" and respectfully disagreeing based on political views or inclinations are largely over. This reflects the entrenchment of the house negro mentality, which demands that everyone remain unified on the "plantation" (plantation thinking in support of the overlord). Those under the sway of this pathology will not tolerate dissent. They aggressively work to ensure that everyone follows the path of a

---

[8] Americans Favor Speech restrictions- https://www.pewresearch.org/short-reads/2023/07/20/most-americans-favor-restrictions-on-false-information-violent-content-online/

[9] American and Guns- https://www.pewresearch.org/short-reads/2024/07/24/key-facts-about-americans-and-guns/

(now-declining) culture dictated by overlords (even if it undermines and prevents personal achievement).

To house negroes, free-thinking and charting one's own path is unacceptable. In today's paradigm, they reject and persecute anyone who refuses to embrace the wretched path paved with the grotesque attributes of Marxism (socialism/communism) and Progressivism. People like me, who dissent based on a well-researched and thorough understanding of the historical disasters precipitated by Marxism and who, therefore, recognize that reckless roads paved with Progressivism inevitably end in disaster, are jeered, rejected, denounced, and castigated. In other words, rejecting Leftist progressivism is simply not tolerated. "Additionally, embracing the house negro pathology requires that the pursuit of faith and the alignment of one's actions and intentions with those foundations be subordinated to the dictates of the 'greater good' (the overlord and plantation). For those trapped in the house negro mindset, God and His Word takes a backseat to prevailing cultural pressures.

Notably, God's Word declares, 'Before I formed you in the womb I knew you, before you were born I set you apart; I appointed you as a prophet to the nations' (Jeremiah 1:5). Yet, people who identify as 'Christian' will gleefully vote for their favorite party that condones killing God's creation (and associated destinies) in the womb. Additionally, in Genesis 1, God creates two biological sexes, male (XY chromosomes) and female (XX chromosomes), yet many Christians will again zealously and gleefully vote for political candidates who assert that there are over 100+ genders. These examples reflect how God

(Faith foundations generally) is being relegated to the background in favor of the 'greater good' dictated by the house negro syndrome.

If we are honest with ourselves, the pathology of the house negro is indeed pervasive. But why? Is it seductive and compelling? Or is it a diabolical mindset driven by compulsion and duress?

There are several reasons why the house negro mindset persists. The most notable is *recompense*. All house negroes are rewarded for maintaining and fulfilling their role. Just as the house negro on the plantation received better treatment, clothing, food, and living conditions, those with the house negro psyche in today's America are well-compensated, receiving better treatment and esteemed positions in education, entertainment, media, politics, and business.

Today's house negroes are celebrated, well-paid in both "hard cash" and "social capital." As long as they continue to "toe the line" of the overlords (mostly anti-American tradition and Marxist) while aggressively castigating any dissenters, they enjoy acceptance, encouragement, wealth, and prestige. They gain money, power, and status at the expense of keeping others under their influence. Their ultimate goal becomes the pursuit of influence and social "cred" rather than breaking free from the overlords and helping others do the same.

With the aggressive house negro pathology pervasive across cultural, political, and familial spheres, many are inclined to succumb to cultural pressures and cower to threats. These individuals reject any desire to dissent out of fear of retribution, fearing cancel culture or disharmony within their families or communities. However, those who fall into this category still fit the description of the house negro syndrome. This syndrome motivates not only those who are paid to keep everyone on the plantation but also those who comply out of fear. Anyone who lacks the desire or willingness to escape the abuse and coercion of the overlord is, wittingly or unwittingly, a house negro and fellow slave who tacitly endorses (by not escaping) the exploits of the house negro.

The bottom line is this: anyone who receives any form of recompense—whether in the form of money, in-kind payments, accelerated status, social credibility, special treatment, or inclusion in the "tribe"—and anyone who acquiesces to avoid the wrath and retribution from the house negro mob (which is also a form of "payment")—is definitively a house negro.

VICTIMOLOGY OF THE HOUSE NEGRO

Another dynamic of life on the plantation that can be gleaned from historical writings is the victimization complex. Individuals who willingly submit to servitude are indeed victimized by the overlord, subjected to taunts and threats from house negroes, and trapped by their own lack of desire to improve their circumstances. Many of these individuals actually embrace their "victim" status. While they endure hardship, they also find solace in pointing to the overlord ("the system") and the abuse from house negroes (in this context, educators, employers, etc., as instruments of the overlords) as the reasons for their perpetual plight. As long as they remain on the plantation, they have excuses for their relative lack of achievement. Rather than freeing themselves, they wallow in their plight, deflecting focus from their own agency by blaming the overlords as oppressors. This mindset uses victimhood as a blanket excuse to justify the lack of accomplishment instead of proactively striving to escape abuse and servitude altogether, leading to a self-destructive cycle.

Those who adopt and cling to the label of "victim" do not free themselves to do more or better; instead, this mindset reinforces their relative servitude and ensures their continued obedience to the overlord. Victimhood, therefore, secures their allegiance to the overlord, while the overlord (the system) actively encourages this allegiance with empty platitudes and by deflecting blame to other offenders. The cycle of abuse and enslavement then continues unabated, perpetuated by the overlord's interest in maintaining the status quo. If this seems illogical, that's because it is. Recognizing the existence of this arcane cycle indicates logical thinking; the entire plantation society premise is fundamentally unprincipled and irrational.

TRIBALISM'S GRIP ON THE HOUSE NEGRO

Due to its corrosive nature, the pathology of the house negro easily becomes a tribal contagion. The contagious sequence begins with the house negro syndrome fostering uniformity in supporting the master/overlord. This syndrome demands conformity in thinking about the overlord (and associated systems). With the demand for obedience, the house negro uniformly rejects any attempts to escape. This sequence enables the spread of the house negro syndrome, which is then informally accepted and embraced with tribal dedication and fervor.

Fervent tribalism becomes the driving force behind actions and intentions, perplexing outside observers. Those who do not conform to the house negro syndrome struggle to understand the zeal and fervor it inspires. It is difficult to grasp a pervasive pathology driven by the base emotion of tribalism, which is not motivated by logic, principles, rationality, morals, or faith. Our understanding deepens when we recognize this syndrome as a pathology entirely beholden to overlords and driven by various forms of recompense. Recompense alone is sufficient motivation and reward to generate a tribal contagion.

The house negro contagion is also spread with tribal fervency across generations. Those who embrace the house negro syndrome today often propagate it to their offspring and future generations by affirming it as a "family tradition," which must be adopted without question. My own family is a good example of this. For generations, my family members have based their voting patterns and beliefs more on tradition than on principles, morals, or even faith foundations. Today, they blindly march to the ballot box, pulling the lever for a political party solely out of 'family tradition' without considering policies, promises, or holding the party accountable. The tribal nature of the house negro syndrome is a contagion without limits. It has persisted throughout generations and will continue to thrive if left unchecked.

This syndrome illustrates that tribalism should no longer be relegated to ancient paradigms. In the context of the house negro syndrome, tribalism is actively encouraged and practiced to this day.

CROSS-DOMAIN INFLUENCES AND THEIR IMPACT

The level of behavioral obedience conferred by way of the house negro pathology brings to mind a quote from Oswald Spengler, German Historian and Philosopher (1880–1936). Oswald mused, "Today we live so cowed under the bombardment of this intellectual artillery that hardly anyone can attain to the inward detachment that is required for a clear view of the monstrous drama. The will-to-power operating under a pure democratic disguise has finished off its masterpiece so well that the object's sense of freedom is actually flattered by the most thorough-going enslavement that has ever existed." This quote profoundly describes how house negroes succumb to sinisterly veiled enslavement while wholly deluded with notions of freedom. The only way to escape would be to escape the stronghold of the pathology. If there is a perceived need or desire to escape its grip, the pathology spreads.

As with all other pathologies, the house negro syndrome is not relegated to the single domain of American politics. In our myriad complex human interactions, we see the syndrome can cross many different domains (or aspects) of life.

Some may demonstrate signs of cultural pressure demanding conformity on their job/workplace (whereby there's unwanted pressure to participate in dinner and drinks with cohorts or clients), or in family/intimate relationships (whereby family members or intimate partners pressure and demand agreement on something that is otherwise not agreeable). Even educational spaces can demand students conform their thinking in order to get a good grade. These scenarios demonstrate that when demands for conformity are made, and those with the house negro pathology are inclined to do something they don't want to do. They fail to exercise independence so they can forestall wrath and retribution from those who make demands. The point is, the house negro syndrome is not confined to the political domain. As a pathology, it can (and most often does) infect people in many domains. Many feel constrained and oppressed by always having to comport themselves in ways that are "performative" and not motivated by the authentic self.

RECONCILING THE HOUSE NEGRO CONDITION

It's abundantly clear that anyone in America can fall under the archetype of a house negro—family, friends, politicians, media personalities, educators, sports figures, athletes, entertainers—anyone! This book helps us identify who they are and offers them help.

Humans can be blinded and unwittingly drawn into almost any paradigm. Once individuals become better observers of themselves and the paradigms they participate in, they can decide to change. House negroes can receive help and change course with the support of others who help them better observe their actions and intentions. Whether they act out of a desire for recompense or an inability to confront and dissent (which is essentially cowardice), they can choose to change.

Observing the syndrome so we can change and reorient ourselves to the freedom and liberty that come with freethinking is what can provide immediate help in changing the trajectory of America.

Two

Inconvenient Contrivances of Life as A Field Negro

Excerpt on the Field Negro from Malcolm X's speech "Message to the Grassroots" delivered in 1963:

"…But then you had another Negro out in the field. The house Negro was in the minority. The masses—the field Negroes were the masses. They were in the majority. When the master got sick, they prayed that he'd die. [Laughter] If his house caught on fire, they'd pray for a wind to come along and fan the breeze.

If someone came to the house Negro and said, "Let's go, let's separate," naturally…he would say "Go where? What could I do without boss? Where would I live? How would I dress? Who would look out for me?" That's the house Negro. But if you went to the field Negro and said, "Let's go, let's separate," he wouldn't

even ask you where or how. He'd say, "Yes, let's go."
And that one ended right there."[10]

The most inconvenient reality for the field negro is recognizing and pursuing the truth of his freedom. This truth is inconvenient because of the slavery and oppression he has endured. It is a contrivance because he is no longer blinded to the fact that he has innate, God-given rights, and that, whether in chains or not, he is free indeed. This is the reality the field negro pursued with unwavering zeal.

Unlike the house negro, who was conditioned to loyalty and submission to the demands of the overlord, the field negro held an opposing perspective. The field negroes mindset was one of rebellion; he rejected oppressive actions and intentions, always seeking ways to escape the abusive tyranny of his oppressors. Although the life of a field negro was fraught with strife and significant challenges, he remained resilient in the face of major obstacles and hardship.

The mindset of the field negroes symbolizes resilience, personal struggle, independence, and an unwavering commitment to challenge and overcome oppressive systems. They typically were fiercely independent, which led house negroes to keep a close eye on them. To the ire of house negroes, field negroes were always inclined toward freedom and constantly plotted ways to escape the plantation, often encouraging others to do the same.

---

10 Speech transcribed via Columbia Univ., https://ccnmtl.columbia.edu/projects/mmt/mxp/speeches/mxa17.html

This rebellious mindset made them easy targets for threats and public humiliation by house negroes, who used these tactics to assert authority and enforce conformity among the field slaves.

Field negroes, especially those deemed "rebellious," were subjected to more work and harsher conditions compared to those who conformed to the dictates of house negroes. Independent-minded field negroes worked longer hours under the blistering sun. This harsh treatment hardened both their bodies and their inner resolve, fueling their determination to escape the grossly unequal conditions of their plight.

The fundamental distinction between the house negro and the field negro: *The house negroes desired comfort and recompense from their master, while the field negroes harbored a deep-seated longing for freedom.* The field negro saw himself as a human being, just as capable as any other, and therefore yearned to be respected and treated as an equal, not as an enslaved and abused individual. He knew that God had given him innate and irrevocable rights to be free, and because he saw his freedom as nonnegotiable, he pursued it with abandon. This heightened awareness, coupled with a rebellious spirit and aversion to subjugation, entrenched a deep desire for freedom within the field negro..

THE FIELD NEGRO MENTALITY: HEROES OF INDEPENDENCE

The mindset of the field negro offers a profound lens through which we can reflect on the heroic actions of historical figures who embodied the resilience and resolve inherent in this spirit.

Sojourner Truth's life perfectly correlates to the mindset

and pathology of the field negro. Sojourner Truth embodied the field negro mindset through her unwavering resilience and fierce commitment to independence. Born into slavery in New York, she endured the brutal realities of field labor, where she endured cruelty and the constant threat of violence, shaping her into a woman of extraordinary strength.[11] This experience fueled her deep sense of resistance and a burning desire for freedom. After escaping with her infant daughter, Truth became a powerful voice against slavery, racism, and sexism, fearlessly confronting oppression. Unlike the house negroes who exacerbated her life as a slave, her field negro mindset was characterized by a deep sense of resistance and a burning desire for freedom; Truth's life and activism were a direct reflection of this mindset.

Truth's life testified to the field negro mindset—unyielding, confrontational, and driven by an unshakeable belief in justice and equality. She lived her life as a warrior for freedom, never compromising her principles and always fighting for the rights of her people, making her an enduring symbol of resistance and empowerment.

The mindset of the field negro is defined by a willingness to take extreme risks in the pursuit of freedom, undeterred by danger. The story of Henry "Box" Brown exemplifies this through his storied, daring escape from slavery in Virginia by mailing himself in a wooden crate to Philadelphia. This bold

---

[11] *Narrative of Sojourner Truth: A Northern Slave,* Sojourner Truth (as told to Olive Gilbert) 1850.

act of resistance highlights the resilience and defiance characteristic of the field negro, making Brown a powerful symbol of unyielding opposition to the system of slavery and oppression.

The most notable historical figures who exemplify the field negro mindset and pathology are the honorable Frederick Douglass and the indomitable heroine Harriet Tubman. They stand as powerful exemplars of Malcolm X's concept of the field negro through their fierce resistance to oppression and unwavering pursuit of freedom. Both Douglass and Tubman endured the brutal conditions of slavery, and rather than succumbing to the tyranny of those who sought to keep them enslaved, they channeled this suffering to fuel their determination to break free and become beacons of hope for others.

Douglass, driven by a relentless desire to be seen as equal and not inherently inferior, devoted himself to mastering reading and writing. Through his eloquent speeches, he exposed the deep injustices of slavery and rose to prominence as a leading voice in the American abolitionist movement. His grace, excellence, and unwavering determination became powerful tools in his fight against the system that sought to dehumanize him.[12]

Harriet Tubman, on the other hand, was propelled by an insatiable determination to escape the shackles of slavery. Not content with securing her freedom, she returned time and again to lead countless others to liberation through the

---

[12] *Narrative of the Life of Frederick Douglass, an American Slave,* Frederick Douglass (1845)- Anti-Slavery Office.

ingenious routes of the Underground Railroad.[13] A fearless risk-taker, Tubman repeatedly placed her life in jeopardy to see others freed from the oppressive and abusive slave systems.

Together, Frederick Douglass and Harriet Tubman stand as monumental examples of the resilience, independence, and active resistance that embody the rebellious spirit of the field negro, as so powerfully described by Malcolm X. From their example and indomitable spirit, Douglass and Tubman continue to inspire hearts and minds of all others who embrace the pathology of the field negro.

Field slaves like Frederick Douglass and Harriet Tubman lived in a world where vigilance was a way of survival, constantly wary of the house negroes who often acted as the eyes and ears of the masters. These house negroes were frequently rewarded for their loyalty and incentivized to keep a close watch on anyone daring to challenge the system of slavery on the plantation. To them, people like Douglass and Tubman were seen as threats, as their rebellious spirits endangered the fragile order of plantation life.

Douglass, known for his unyielding defiance and daring acts of resistance, quickly became a figure of suspicion. His attempts to break free from the chains of slavery were not his only acts of rebellion; they were a declaration of war against the oppressive status quo. Each failed escape only hardened his resolve, and with every setback, his resentment toward

---

[13] *Harriet Tubman: The Road to Freedom*, Catherine Clinton (2004). Little, Brown and Company.

the house negroes grew. They were not just enforcers of the masters' will—they were symbols of the betrayal that festered within the enslaved community. In Douglass's eyes, their allegiance to the overlords was an affront to the struggle for freedom, and his disdain for them was as deep as his desire to escape.

"GIVE THE NEGRO NOTHING EXCEPT FAIR PLAY!"

Frederick Douglass, in one of his most powerful speeches, articulated his deep-seated distrust of the oppressive systems that sought to control and manipulate African Americans. His uncompromising message was clear: the best thing anyone could do for African American slaves was to simply "let them alone." In his words:

"I have but one theory in regard to the negro, and that seems to be conceded, by Democrats as well as Republicans. It is summed up in one word—Let him alone! That is about your whole duty in regard to the negro—to let him alone. You want to be doing something for him and with him; and your doing something for us, with us and by us has played the mischief with us already (applause); and what we most need at this time is to be let alone. My politics in regard to the negro is simply this: Give him fair play and let him alone, but be sure you give him fair play. He is now a man before the law. I rejoice at it. What we want, what we are

*resolved to have, is the right to be men among men;
men everywhere."*[14]

Frederick Douglass's philosophy of "rugged individualism" was not formed in a vacuum. His fierce independence and desire to be left to his own devices were shaped by the betrayals he suffered at the hands of those closest to the masters—the house slaves. These individuals, willing to report and betray their fellow slaves, often led to Douglass's capture. These experiences only deepened his disdain for any system that sought to control or meddle in the lives of black men and women. Douglass firmly believed that the government's only proper role was to free people to pursue happiness on their own terms. In his view, to be truly "free," people had to be left alone, unencumbered by oppressive structures or government oversight.

Douglass was so adamant in this belief that he rejected the notions of reparations or handouts. His experiences taught him that house slaves, rewarded for their loyalty, often lost their souls to the dictates of the overlords. In Douglass's mind, if the government provided handouts or compensation, it could become a new kind of overlord, and those receiving these benefits might undermine their humanity by deferring to the will of the government.

Douglass was unwavering in his commitment to personal achievement based on merit and individualism. In another of his famous speeches, he reiterated and confirmed his resolve:

---

[14] Douglass In his Own Words, https://www.cato.org/commentary/frederick-douglass-was-own-man

"Everybody has asked the question, 'What shall we do with the Negro?' I have had but one answer from the beginning: Do nothing with us! Your doing with us has already played the mischief with us. Do nothing with us! If the apples will not remain on the tree of their own strength, if they are worm-eaten at the core, if they are early ripe and disposed to fall, let them fall! I am not for tying or fastening them on the tree in any way, except by nature's plan, and if they will not stay there, let them fall. And if the Negro cannot stand on his own legs, let him fall also. All I ask is, give him a chance to stand on his own legs! Let him alone!"

A consistent refrain in Frederick Douglass's rhetoric is the desire to be left alone. This yearning is a primary tenet of the field slave's experience. The unyielding desire for unencumbered freedom—to pursue personal ambitions without restraint, to serve God in whatever way one deems best, and to simply be free from aggression and interference—are fundamental motivations for field slaves. This mindset reveals a deep-seated drive for autonomy and self-determination, central to their identity and struggles.

THE LONE RANGER SYNDROME: INDEPENDENCE AT ALL COSTS

Courage in the face of grim circumstances and oppression—the willingness to confront immense and abusive structures and systems—requires tremendous strength. To risk one's life to escape corrosive mindsets, demands for conformity and obedience, and blatant injustices can be a profoundly lonely journey. While the collective spirit driving past heroes to demand freedom showcases incredible bravery and determination, the mindset of field slaves also harbors a potential downside. This mindset is closely linked to what can be described as the "Lone Ranger Syndrome."[15]

In the context of field slaves, the Lone Ranger Syndrome becomes evident in their relentless "never give up" ambitions. Field slaves were always on the lookout for an escape; it became a passion that consumed them until they successfully broke free.

Field slaves were inherently distrustful of others, especially house slaves who were ever-present on the plantation. House slaves, who had no desire to escape, were often seen as obstacles or threats to freedom. This pervasive distrust led field slaves to keep to themselves, internalizing their ambitions and relying solely on their own resolve. This is typical of the Lone Ranger Syndrome, where the individual prefers to act independently, seeking neither encouragement nor acknowledgment from others.

A defining trait of lone rangers is their longing for new horizons, embracing uncertainties as opportunities. While other slaves couldn't imagine life in the "free world" without the support or oversight of their masters or some system of control,

---

[15] "Are You a Lone Ranger?" *Isabel Cabrera | May 3, 2024*, https://experteditor.com.au/blog/are-you-a-lone-ranger-signs-you-have-a-fiercely-independent-personality/

field slaves relished the idea of an uncertain life in freedom. They were confident that, whatever the circumstance, they possessed the inner resolve to prevail and overcome any situation.

Compared to house slaves, the personalities of field slaves were often seen as quirky and unpredictable. Lone rangers are known for working independently and doing things differently, often preferring no support, supervision, or need for collaboration. In the context of field slaves, this Lone Ranger mentality was expressed in their desire to be left to themselves—to simply be left alone.

NAVIGATING INCONVENIENCES OF "LONE RANGERISM"

While field slaves exhibited a "Lone Ranger" mindset—a psychology characterized by admirable qualities like independence, determination, and self-reliance, it was sometimes wrought inconvenience. While most traits were positive and instrumental in helping them plan and execute escapes, this mindset also carried significant downsides.

One of the most notable drawbacks of embracing this Lone Ranger mentality was the inability to confide in others. The pervasive distrust of those around them, particularly in the treacherous environment of the plantation, led to isolation. This isolation often left field slaves feeling lonely, disconnected, and potentially depressed. However, given the immense ambition and zeal required to escape, it's likely that any feelings of depression were fleeting rather than persistent.

The inherent distrust that fueled field slaves' independence could also foster paranoia. This mindset, while sometimes necessary for survival, could be counterproductive. Paranoia might lead to chaotic or poorly conceived escape plans, preventing the development of coherent strategies. Paranoia is not a personal trait that helps foster success.

Frederick Douglass's life illustrated how a Lone Ranger's strong sense of independence could sometimes translate into stubbornness or an unwillingness to adapt. This rigidity made it difficult to change course or pivot when circumstances demanded a different approach. Field slaves who stubbornly clung to delusions of escape—without reason or confirmation—could find themselves trapped by their own inflexibility.

However, the inconveniences stemming from the Lone Ranger mindset and the field slave's determination were simply the price of freedom—a price well worth paying. This mindset has given the world an incredible legacy of heroes and heroines whose courage and resolve continue to inspire.

Three

Unveiling the Overlord

THE "HUSTLE AND FLOW" OF PLANTATION OVERLORDS

Historical books provide insight into life on the plantation. Books from Frederick Douglass, like "My Bondage, My Freedom," not only reveal the nature and context of the house negro and field negro, but go further to provide insight into the psyche of the overlord.

From historical description, it is easy to conclude the psyche of an overlord is brutish, unrelenting, maniacal, and malevolent. Overlords feel entitled and will do anything to cement what they view as their 'highly esteemed' and entitled position.

Fundamentally, an overlord covets the idea of 'being on top,' 'the master,' and the boss of everyone. They see themselves as important, elite, and masterminds of all, destined for greatness. History confirms overlords were responsible for the plantation and maintained ultimate power over all slaves through sheer force and control, and if necessary, using torment to keep everyone in fear and under their command. In a sense, they acted like pimps.

Years ago, actor Terrence Howard starred in the 2005 film "Hustle and Flow," which tells the story of a Memphis street pimp who transforms his illicit lifestyle into a successful rap career. In the film, Howard's character exerts control over everyone in his environment, using manipulation and cunning to maintain power, with little regard for the well-being of those around him.

When juxtaposed with the archetype of a plantation overlord, the pimp's character reveals striking similarities. Fundamentally, both the pimp and the overlord are driven by a desire to be "on top," seeing themselves as elite figures destined for greatness. The overlord, responsible for the plantation, wields ultimate authority over the slaves, maintaining control through fear and brutality. By leveraging influence and manipulation, especially through figures like house negroes, the overlord ensures the continued subjugation of the enslaved.

Both the pimp and the overlord share a pathology marked by a lack of empathy and a disregard for human suffering. Their primary goal is the pursuit of power and control, often justified by a belief that the ends justify the means. This mindset allows them to dismiss their brutal actions as necessary, as they exploit ethical boundaries to maintain their dominance. Their narcissistic drive is rooted in a desire for legacy—whether through wealth, dynasties, or shaping the world according to their vision. Unlike others who see themselves as part of a community, these figures view themselves as world changers, driven by the egoistic and prideful delusion of grandeur that fuels their quest for power. Clearly sociopathic.

THE SOULLESS SOCIOPATHY OF THE OVERLORD

The pathology of the overlord is inherently sociopathic, loathsome, and antisocial, embracing a dark and twisted force that drives them to dismiss the God-given rights of others. Their sociopathy reveals itself in their blatant disregard for human dignity, marked by a chilling lack of empathy, remorse, or moral conscience. In their decadence, they revel in malevolence, taking perverse pleasure in the suffering of others.

The overlord's mindset is fueled by an inflated sense of self-importance, a grandiose belief that they are destined for greatness. This delusion often leads them to justify any action, no matter how immoral, as necessary for achieving their vision. To that end, they act ruthlessly, wielding physical, emotional, and psychological weapons with precision. Exploitation becomes a tool, fear a currency, and violence a means to enforce their oppressive schemes. They do not hesitate to administer harsh punishments, public humiliation, and other cruelties to keep others in submission. These actions confirm that the overlord syndrome is often irrational and soulless.

Overlord archetypes operate within a dangerous psychosis that allows them to transition seamlessly from being a loving family member within their home to an inconsolable, brutish tyrant in the fields. They exploit and abuse others without a trace of remorse. This duality grants them a twisted sense of justification, even as they degrade and oppress. Every action they take is carefully synchronized, designed to dissuade, disempower, and demoralize. These actions spread like cancer, devouring the very essence of the soul. In essence, those operating under the spell of overlord syndrome possess a twisted psyche that fuels sociopathic behaviors, taking pleasure in degrading and demoralizing innocent lives.

Human flourishing, encompassing mind, body, and spirit, begins in the soul. The sociopath who embraces the overlord psyche seeks to undermine human dignity and the flourishing of the soul, relishing in the abuse and subjugation of others as a means of imposing their will. Their actions, driven by depravity, echo the evil, satanic intentions in John 10:10: "The thief comes only to steal, kill and destroy…" The overlord, like the thief, embodies these malevolent forces, motivated by a desire to steal destinies, kill the soul, and destroy any possibility of human flourishing.

REFLECTIONS OF THE OVERLORD THROUGH THE "REAR VIEW" OF FREDERICK DOUGLASS

Through his seminal writings and speeches—*Narrative of the Life of Frederick Douglass, an American Slave*,[16] *My Bondage and My Freedom*, [17] *The Meaning of July Fourth for the Negro,*

---

[16] Narrative of the Life of Frederick Douglass, an American Slave (1845), Anti-Slavery Office (Boston)

[17] My Bondage and My Freedom (1855), Miller, Orton & Mulligan (Auburn and Buffalo, New York)

and *Lectures on American Slavery*—Frederick Douglass offers profound insights into the insidious motivations and actions of the overlord.

Douglass reveals that overlords were not mere figures of authority but embodiments of cruelty and domination. The overlord's ambition extended beyond the mere extraction of labor; he harbored an insatiable desire to crush spirits, dehumanize individuals, and assert control over the very souls of slaves. His power was not earned through merit or benevolence but through fear, violence, and the relentless exploitation of those he deemed inferior.

The overlord fancied himself a master of men, yet he was enslaved by his own arrogance and depravity. He used the whip and chain as instruments of terror, believing that sheer force could bend others to his will. In his tyranny, he exposed his true nature—cowardly, insecure, and incapable of recognizing the inherent dignity in each human being.

To the overlord, slaves were not individuals but property—objects to be used, traded, and discarded at his whim. He considered himself superior, but in reality, he was imprisoned by his own hatred and ignorance. His world was built on lies, maintained through violence, and destined to collapse under the weight of its own inhumanity.

The overlord is an enemy of freedom and a stain on the conscience of any society that tolerates his rule.

While we have moved beyond the era of plantations and overt chattel slavery depicted by Douglass, the pathology of the overlord persists in more subtle forms. Today, the most pervasive (though often hidden) manifestations of overlordism are embedded in laws and policies that subtly perpetuate this pathology on a global scale. This means that the overlord archetype remains, to some extent, ubiquitous and inescapable.

X MARKS MARX: IDEOLOGICAL BATTLEFIELDS

The most imposing force shaping America's political landscape is driven by masterminds who fully embody the archetype of the overlord. Though this influence is fundamentally global, its direct impact on American politics is profound.

Ironically, the most influential overlord ideology embraced and propagated worldwide originates from one of the most unaccomplished, diabolical miscreants in human history—Karl Marx. As a philosophy, Marxism dominates as the most pervasive and grotesque pathology, deeply embedded in the mindset of today's overlords.

In his March 12, 1964, speech titled "The Ballot or the Bullet," Malcolm X declared, "I don't see any need for any such thing as Marxism. The black man doesn't have to be a Marxist to be free." Despite the promises of greater freedom and opportunity for black people, Malcolm X was wary of Marxism. He believed that its authoritarian and totalitarian tendencies could dilute or undermine the specific goals of the black community for unrestricted freedom. Malcolm X recognized that the motivations behind global communist movements could compromise the pursuit of black empowerment through independence and self-determination—and he was right.

As an overarching ideology, Marxism, when viewed through

the lens of the "overlord syndrome," has profoundly influenced global upheaval, often leading to outcomes that restrict freedom and exacerbate human suffering. Every country or society that has embraced Marxism—whether in the form of socialism or communism—has experienced economic and societal collapse. Marx's sociopathic tendencies, as expressed through his ideology, consistently result in less freedom, greater poverty, and widespread despair.

Marx's ideology laid the foundation for social revolutions aimed at dismantling all existing power structures—family, religion, education, media, politics, and particularly capitalism. While free markets and capitalism, despite their imperfections, offer individuals opportunities for human flourishing and freedom, Marxism seeks to restrict that freedom. This is a poignant way in which Marxism (an overarching pathology) embodies the archetype of the overlord. The overlord syndrome experienced through Marxism inculcates the traits and characteristics of the overlord syndrome and, therefore, poses a danger and threat to everyone.

It is easy to recognize and then steer clear of activity street pimps; what they do (as an overlord) doesn't impact you and can be avoided. But it is impossible to avoid and escape a diabolical syndrome secreted and expressed through entrenched global Marxist mindsets. When this global ideology takes root, the overlord syndrome manifests itself and is tyrannically exercised over everyone.

The overlord pathology intertwined in Marxist ideologies has been used to justify the control and manipulation of entire societies. Communist regimes, inspired by Marxist ideology, often centralized power in the hands of a ruling elite or party, exercising control over the economy, politics, and the lives of citizens. These regimes, authoritarian and totalitarian by nature, concentrated power in a few hands, fully demonstrating the embodiment of the overlord archetype.

The outcomes of todays Marxist-inspired regimes mirror the oppression and control of plantation overlords of old. The pathological connection and correlation between Marx's theories and the pathology of overlords is manifest!

DOUGLASS VERSUS MARX: PROFOUND CHARACTERS IN PERPETUAL IDEOLOGICAL CONFLICT

Like Malcolm X, Frederick Douglass was also suspicious of Karl Marx and Marxism, viewing Marxist ideologies as a significant threat to the freedom he and others had worked so valiantly to secure.

Although Douglass and Marx were born in the same year (1818), they had little else in common and were starkly contrasted in their beliefs and values. After understanding that all men were created equal, Douglass used this principle to fuel his determination to escape from slavery. He recognized that merit, self-reliance, economic independence, and individual rights were vital for building the personal dignity of African Americans. This mindset was the opposite of the "overlord syndrome" expressed through Marxist ideology, which advocates for collective ownership and the dismantling of all existing hegemonic systems, particularly capitalism.

Douglass's primary focus was on the abolition of slavery and the rights of African Americans, centering his activism around freedom and racial equality. In contrast, Marx focused on class struggle and economic inequality (mostly through Union activism in workplaces), rejecting the notion of innate God-given freedom for all humankind. Douglass understood that Marxism's emphasis on class struggle did not adequately address the specific demands for freedom and equality for black people. He viewed Marxism as creating a distinct form of oppression through the commands of a dominant authority (and its associated "masterminds"), too inflexible in its analysis of social classes, and not focused enough on the atrocities of slavery, personal freedoms, and ethical concerns of all individuals.

Douglass's personal experiences as a former slave (field negro) and his understanding of American society shaped his worldview. He found that Marxist theories, which were developed in a European context, did not translate well to the American context, particularly in addressing slavery and related racial issues.

The stark contrast between Douglass and Marx was not only evident in economic and social domains but also in matters of faith. Douglass knew and feared God, and he was an ordained minister. Conversely, Marx despised the notion of God, famously asserting his goal to "dethrone God (and destroy capitalism)." Additionally, in one of his poems, Marx poetically declared, "Thus Heaven I've forfeited, I know it full well. My soul, once true to God, is chosen for Hell," indicating a stark divergence in spiritual outlook.[18] While Douglass embodied faith and moral integrity, Marx's writings indicate the opposite; he embraced a worldview that (no doubt) Douglass (and his contemporaries) saw as reprobate and derelict. Unlike Douglass, Marx starkly suggests through his many actions and deeds that he was a hellion and demoniac!

The most telling contrast between Marx and Douglass arises when comparing their backgrounds: Douglass was born into American slavery, and Marx was born in Germany and eventually became part of the European elite. Douglass viewed capitalism as the primary path for former slaves to achieve freedom, liberty, and wealth. In contrast, Marx abhorred such notions, advocating for an ideology that eschews personal freedoms and wealth in deference to the dictates of the state (masterminds who lord over nations).

Frederick Douglass understood the significance of God-given talents, skills, and abilities. He encouraged hard work, personal responsibility, and the ownership of property and land as the ultimate pursuit of freedom. He stated, "To own the soil is no harm in itself. It is right that [man] should own it. It is his duty to possess it— and to possess it in that way in which its energies and properties can be made most useful to the human family—now and always.[19]

---

[18] Karl Marx Interview – https://www.3-16am.co.uk/blog/exclusive-3-16-interview-with-karl-marx

[19] Douglass speech- https://frederickdouglassanthology.georgetown.domains/post/the-freedmens-monument-to-abraham-lincoln/

The contrasting archetypes of Frederick Douglass and Karl Marx provide a compelling comparison between the mindsets of the field negro and the overlord. Douglass embodied the mindset and drive of a field negro; he rejected being lorded over by anyone and was insatiably desirous of exercising his innate God-given independence and freedom. His life and achievements were dedicated to ensuring that everyone could experience the same mindset toward freedom, the mindset and pathology of a field negro!

Karl Marx, on the other hand, had the mindset of a privileged elitist—an overlord. Despite his lack of notable personal accomplishments (he was a perpetually unemployed serial adulterer, womanizer, misogynist, alcoholic, and racist/eugenicist), Marx promoted ideologies that entrenched the belief that all men are not equal, asserting that elites are the masterminds who should be in charge while the rest are "plebs" who must serve the interest of "the State" (i.e., plebs are to be subservient to big government nation-states). Marx rejected individual rights, personal responsibility, and free-market economies, instead advocating for planned economies and societies where overlords control resources and freedoms. Unfortunately, the overlord syndrome intertwined via the grotesque ideologies of Marxism has metastasized into a pervasive global issue that we are battling to this day.

Based on the wisdom gleaned from the experiences of Frederick Douglass and Malcolm X, Karl Marx and Marxism are seen as oppressive, torturous, and debilitating to human flourishing. If we were to express this assessment in modern terms,

Marxism could be likened to a "plantation pimp," an insatiable overlord seeking to devour entire nations, not just individual human souls.

Marxism, the pervasive ideology of the overlord, is brutish, intolerant, and restrictive of personal freedoms. It denies human dignity and corrodes the soul, impeding human flourishing. It is especially troubling to witness this sociopathic ideology being embraced and spreading so rampantly across the globe. This harsh reality of Marxism demands personal introspection from each individual.

The rise of Marxism (manifesting as the "overlord syndrome") is made possible only through the dutiful allegiance of those who embrace the house negro syndrome. These individuals are compensated with money, global influence, "social cred," and the comfort of being celebrated instead of "canceled" (via cancel culture).

MINDSETS OF ESCAPE OR CAPTIVITY: THE ETERNAL QUESTION

The fundamental difference between house negroes and field negroes lies in the notion of captivity. House negroes are 'captured'—committing their heart, mind, and soul to the dictates of the overlords, regardless of conflicts with their personal morals, faith foundation or principles. This pathology functions as a psychosis, allowing them to reconcile with the demands of those who hold power over them. If the overlord system is Marxist, authoritarian, or totalitarian, the house negro will embrace it. Even when overlords espouse blatantly racist ideologies—like those of the KKK or neo-Nazi movements—while hypocritically proclaiming justice and equality, the house negro will still comply. This is the nature of their captivity. Captured individuals surrender their logic, principles, and morals, casting them aside in blind obedience to the dictates of their masters.

This phenomenon is pervasive in American society, where many have been captured by overlords promoting rampant Marxism and globalism. The result? Not only are individuals captured, but America itself has also fallen under this domination.

On the other hand, the antidote to this is found in those who operate under the pathology of the field negro. These individuals are untethered and cannot be tamed. They possess a mindset of escape, seeking freedom from groupthink, cultural pressures, and authoritarian structures. They fight against anything that threatens to control their speech or actions. Field negroes, like Frederick Douglass, Sojourner Truth and Harriet Tubman, embrace their God-given rights and embody a spirit of resilience and freedom.

Sadly, many fail to recognize the wisdom provided by examples like Douglass, Tubman, and Malcolm X, falling prey to the dangers of captivity by Marxist overlords. Lacking the will or desire to escape, they succumb to the life of enduring the pathology of a house negro, prisoners to their own complacency.

Now that these archetypes have been revealed, it's time to ask yourself: where do you stand in the American political landscape? Are you an overlord, a house negro, or do you possess the mindset of freedom like Douglass and Tubman, true field negroes? The distinctions between these archetypes are clear. So, 'Which one are you?'"

Four

Real-Time Overlord Domination

OVERLORDS AND THEIR HOLD OVER SOCIETY

Malcolm X was prescient in popularizing characterizations of the overlord, house negro and field negro and using these sharp and powerful parallels between the brutal conditions of slavery and the ongoing oppressive structures in America.

Malcolm X frequently spoke of the oppressive systems and individuals who perpetuated racism, likening them to the plantation overlords who once wielded unchecked power over enslaved black people. To Malcolm, the relationship between the enslaved and the plantation overlord was one of unrelenting dominance, enforced submission, and psychological manipulation. The overlord wasn't merely a figure of the past; he was the embodiment of a systemic pathology of tyranny and exploitation that persisted in Malcolm's present-day America. While Malcolm's parallels may have been viewed as over-prescribed and "simplistic" because he was African American and possibly overly sympathetic to the plight of black slaves, his parallels are proving prescient as they neatly overlay onto the lived experience and plight of every American today.

Through vivid imagery and unflinching honesty, Malcolm X paints the picture of house negroes and field negroes, and then provides a vibrant understanding of the motivations and intent of the plantation overlord. He describes the plantation overlord as a rather insecure figure who maintained control through violence and fear, keeping the enslaved in a perpetual state of dependency and ignorance. Malcolm urged his audience to recognize that this overlord as a type of character and mindset was not confined to history books but was alive and working within the systemic structures that continued to oppress people. Understanding this history, Malcolm insisted, was crucial to combatting the ongoing legacy of the plantation overlord in contemporary society.

In today's world, we see the echoes and reverberations of the overlord syndrome at work via pervasive ideologies and systems that threaten human freedom and dignity. Marxism, with its global reach and totalitarian tendencies, is a system and ideology likened to the modern-day overlord—a continuation of the same pathology that once fueled the brutality of the plantation. Like the overlords of old, Marxism is abusive, corrosive, and authoritarian. It is a force that stifles the expression of inalienable freedoms and human rights on a global scale, and it is the culmination of the overlord pathology that prevents global human flourishing. I would say it this way: Marxism in practice today always establishes slavery.

While the words "Marxism" and "socialism" may seem benign, they pave the path to a form of slavery that we now politely call communism. Socialism refers to the organization of society in such a way that the government owns and controls all means of production and services and aims to "redistribute wealth." Communism, envisions a society without money, private enterprise, or individual property rights—where all economic decisions are made by government-controlled masterminds.[20] These systems overlap in several critical ways: the government controls most or all economic activity, private property is discouraged or eliminated, the nuclear family is viewed as exploitative, and personal aspirations must yield to the dictates of politicians and bureaucrats.[21] Said differently, Marxism is systemically designed to enslave the masses ("plantation negroes"), using their hard work, taxes and other added value, for the benefit of overlords.

Although Marx envisioned a society without government, the reality is that implementing and maintaining his utopian vision requires compulsion and coercion by a powerful state.

---

[20] Idealistic communists even today may insist that in a communist society, all decisions are made by the people voting whether as a whole or in committees, and no central government exists. That concept falls apart in theory and fails whenever attempted. Communist-inspired societies always install powerful governments needed to top-down control economies when market systems are absent. Democide and/or economic collapse, inevitably follow.

[21] *See* Ludwig von Mises, *Planned Chaos* (1972), full text at https://mises.org/mises-daily/planned-chaos; Allen Gindler, "Socialism: A Brief Taxonomy" (2020), full text at https://mises.org/mises-wire/socialism-brief-taxonomy; Jonathan Newman, "Why Do Socialists Hate Families?" (2019), full text at https://mises.org/mises-wire/why-do-socialists-hate-families

A Marxist government by design will enslave, not ensure freedom, and both Frederick Douglass and Malcolm X correctly perceived its corrosively enslaving pathology.

Lysander Spooner, the American abolitionist and political philosopher, captured the essence of innate human freedom when he said, "A man's natural rights are his own, against the whole world; and any infringement of them is equally a crime, whether committed by one man, or by millions; whether committed by one man, calling himself a robber, or by millions, calling themselves a government." While it's unclear whether Frederick Douglass or Malcolm X were directly influenced by Spooner, they certainly echoed the fervent sentiment of his statement.

The mindset of the field negro, as described by Malcolm X, serves as a governor against the onslaught of myriad assaults from Marxist overlords. Because of this, those who resist, who embody the spirit of the field negro, are relentlessly chided and attacked by those who seek to maintain the oppressive status quo of the State (global overlords).

Much evidence confirms global overlords are advancing swiftly, as the spread of communism is accelerating at an alarming rate. If this process continues uncountable people around the world will inevitably find themselves under the control of unelected global masters—powerful policymakers sustained by the unaccountable largesse of global taxpayers and compliant masses. Today's "master-class" of overlords is composed of an oligarchy of billionaires, politicians, corporate CEOs, and technocrats, all wielding immense power over the lives of billions.

The trajectory of nation-states capitulating to authoritarian ideologies and the associated pathology embraced by overlords follows the grand scheme of Karl Marx.

THE SUBJUGATION TACTICS OF KARL MARX

It is difficult to fathom how entire countries built on foundations of freedom (like the United States) can ultimately succumb to the embrace of wretched ideologies that openly reject freedoms.

It's baffling. How did Marxism, an ideology born from a grotesque failure of a human being, achieve global momentum and acceptance? But, alas, we have arrived at this point when grotesque failures are celebrated and persist. Failure to uplift humanity is precisely the legacy of Karl Marx and Marxism.

During his lifetime, Karl Marx was an abject failure in all of his endeavors (personally and professionally). However, he was zealous. He was driven by delusions of grandeur and a pathological desire for world dominance, so he relentlessly pursued his ideological ambitions.

In my book, *Woked Up!*, I summarize Karl Marx's background as follows:

Born on May 5, 1818, to a Jewish family, Marx rejected God and any notion of a Supreme Being at an early age. Despite being a privileged elitist, Marx audaciously raged against capitalism. In college, he was viewed as an unserious student, relying entirely on his parents' financial support instead of working. Marx never held a real job during his lifetime and was a serial grifter, content to mooch off friends and family. Although he asserted "workers' rights," he failed to live up to his own convictions. As historian Paul Johnson explained in his book *Intellectuals* (1988): *"In his own household ... Helen Demuth [the lifelong family maid] ... got her keep but was paid nothing ... She was a ferociously hard worker, not only cleaning and scrubbing but managing the family budget ... Marx never paid her a penny ... In 1849–50 ... [Helen] became Marx's mistress and conceived a child ... Marx refused to acknowledge his responsibility, then or ever, and flatly denied the rumors that he was the father... Friedrich Engels, his longtime financial and intellectual collaborator, claimed the child to save Marx from embarrassment and social fallout that would have surely ensued from his excessive adulterous actions. Helen indeed became Marx's on-demand sex outlet. Marx was the ultimate pathetic and loathsome soul who exemplified sexism and misogyny in his own life."*

Wokcd Upl continues: "Marx was also a physical wreck, suffering from debilitating, festering boils that covered most of his body for decades. He was known for his horrible body odor and neglect of personal hygiene. Emotionally and physically, Marx presented himself as a madman."

Marx's life is the embodiment of the overlord pathology—severely lacking and unaccomplished, yet, through ego and hubris, he felt entitled and elitist, displaying a decadent supe-riority complex. Despite his wretched life, much of the world has now seemingly acquiesced to his ideology. All globalist ex-ploits comport to Marxism. Why is this ideology now accepted? Because his economic philosophy provides a worldview that "morally" justifies mechanisms to centralize power and control (authoritarian and totalitarian), allowing overlords to dominate others.[22]

Today, Marx's ideologies are evident in the rise of global oligarchs, cabals, and elites who dominate vast sectors of the economy, politics, and media. These modern-day overlords control significant portions of the world's wealth and resources at the expense of the broader population.

Global oligarchs—billionaires and powerful corporate lead-ers—wield influence that transcends national borders, shaping government policies, manipulating markets, and controlling key industries. Their wealth and power have reached unprec-edented levels, creating a situation where a small group of indi-viduals and global entities holds sway over the global economy and political systems.

These global overlords—whether they are tech giants, financial moguls, or political elites—reject the principles that promote human flourishing: free markets, personal

---

[22] Vice presidential candidate Tim Walz openly praised socialism, for example, when he said: "One person's socialism is another person's neighborliness." Only total ignorance, or corrupt intention to deceive, could utter such a horrific lie. (Source: https://www.realclearpolitics.com/video/2024/08/06/gov_tim_walz_on_white_dudes_for_kamala_harris_call_one_persons_socialism_is_another_persons_neighborliness.html)

freedoms, meritocracy, and true equality of opportunity. Instead, while they position themselves as protectors of democracy, they enforce a form of 'mobocracy' that serves their interests and ensures their perpetual power and control. They depend on "captured" mobs to do their bidding and ensure their demands are enforced through strict obedience to dictates. The pathology of the house negro is vital to this effort.

MEDIA MOBS: THE OVERLORDS' COMPLICIT SOLDIERS

In the grand narrative of history, the "overlord" archetype emerges time and again as figures who, driven by an insatiable thirst for power, wield immense influence over socio-cultural, political, and economic systems. In our modern era, these overlords are not merely characters in a distant past but living, breathing individuals and institutions that subtly, yet profoundly, shape the world around us. Operating behind the scenes, they pull the strings of policies, manipulate markets, and steer public opinion by controlling cultural trends. They stand above and apart from the struggles of the house negro and field negro archetypes, positioning themselves above the fray, and manipulating the social landscape to serve their own interests.

Consider figures like Bill Gates, Jeff Bezos, Mark Zuckerberg, and George Soros—modern-day overlords who, through their actions and intentions, exemplify this mindset. These individuals command vast resources and wield unparalleled influence over global markets, technology, and communication channels. Their reach extends to every corner of the world, where they often set agendas that impact millions of lives. In many ways, they are the architects of the present, designing a world that reflects their vision and, ultimately, serves their interests.

Individuals or groups who operate behind the scenes in politics—such as lobbyists, major donors, or influential advisors—also embody the overlord archetype. These actors pull the strings on policy decisions, often with little accountability, shaping legislation to steer entire nations.

Owners of major media conglomerates, like Rupert Murdoch (Fox News) or Bob Iger Disney/ABC) are modern-day overlords as well. They control vast networks of information, shaping public discourse and influencing societal norms and political views on a global scale.

In the economic realm, entities like the International Monetary Fund (IMF), the World Bank, World Economic Forum (WEF) or major hedge funds should also be considered overlords. Their decisions and policies can dictate the economic fates of entire countries, with little to no regard for additional hardships and other realities faced by the populations they affect. For example, the WEF now admits the truth about Covid as one researcher described: "It was a 'Test' of our obedience to rapidly forming new world order." [23]

Large pharmaceutical companies like Pfizer, Moderna, and

---

[23] WEF finally Tells The Truth- https://www.thegatewaypundit.com/2024/09/world-economic-forum-finally-tells-truth-about-covid/

Johnson & Johnson that hold monopolies over essential drugs and vaccines also embody the overlord archetype. Their pricing and distribution decisions can mean life or death for millions, underscoring their immense power over global health. And with help from the World Health Organization (WHO), the ability to control narratives (some dangerous and false) about vaccines, vaccines' effectiveness, and respective necessity, is unsurmountable.

These overlords operate with a level of autonomy and influence that often places them beyond the reach of typical checks and balances, making them a potent force in the modern world. What motivates their actions? Influence, power, and control—the same forces that drove plantation overlords of the past and Neo-Marxists of today. There is a significant difference between slaves on the plantation of the past, and global citizens of today, however. Historically, slaves could hope to possibly escape plantations to evade oppressive and abusive overlords. Today, however, the pervasive nature of global oppressive structures and systems means there is no easy escape from such power and control. The overlord syndrome is systemic.

Globalist organizations like the World Economic Forum (WEF), under the leadership of figures like Klaus Schwab and Yuval Noah Harari, promote a Marxist globalist agenda that undermines national sovereignty and human dignity. The International Monetary Fund (IMF), through its austerity measures and economic policies, impose forms of global control that stifle the autonomy of developing nations and diminish the potential for human flourishing. These few examples reveal a pattern of global Marxist entities promoting widespread schemes for universal control, which have been embraced and adopted around the world.

At the heart of the globalist mindset is a belief that these elites are the masterminds destined to reshape the world. To them, the ordinary citizens of the world are merely obstacles to be managed or, more cynically, expendable resources. This worldview justifies a range of coercive measures—whether through forced vaccinations, labor, depopulation schemes, monetary policies, government changes, or social engineering. Each of these actions is seen not as an affront to human liberty, but as necessary steps towards a more "ordered" world, where control rests in the hands of these self-appointed masters or overlords.[24].

In their pursuit of this vision, global overlords sacrifice the principles of individual freedom and human dignity, trading them for a cold, calculated form of order. This order, however, is not one of true peace or prosperity, but of subjugation and control, a stark contrast to the flourishing that is possible when individuals are free to pursue their own paths, unfettered by the designs of those who believe they know better.

It is particularly troubling to recognize that global overlords aggregate, consolidate and enhance their power, control and abusive forms of oppression (primarily) through mobs of those who embrace the pathology of house negroes. These favor-seeking pawns willingly subordinate their morals, ethics,

---

[24] Thomas Sowell explored their vision and methods in *The Vision of the Annointed* (1995).

principles, and faith foundations in order to do their part in manipulating others to uphold "the greater good." As mentioned earlier, ultimately, they are compensated and somehow (ironically) smitten by close association with the money and power of those who dictate and lord over them (overlords). Since their hearts and minds are rooted in plantation pathology and captured, they cannot see their dereliction; therefore, it is almost impossible for them to break free from their compliant captivity.

THE OVERLORDS' "MOBOCRACY": MEDIA MOB AS THE HOUSE NEGRO

"We are grateful to The Washington Post, The New York Times, Time Magazine and other great publications whose directors have attended our meetings and respected their promises of discretion for almost forty years... It would have been impossible for us to develop our plan for the world if we had been subjected to the bright lights of publicity during those years. But, the world is now more sophisticated and prepared to march towards a world government. The supranational sovereignty of an intellectual elite and world bankers is surely preferable to the national autodetermination practiced in past centuries." ~David Rockefeller from a speech at a Bilderberg meeting in 1991[25]

---

[25] DavidRockerfellerQuote-https://www.goodreads.com/quotes/288636-we-are-grateful-to-the-washington-post-the-new-york

David Rockefeller's words reveal a strategic and deliberate collusion with the media. Where journalism was once heralded as the voice of the people, it has now become today's overlords most powerful and notorious tool.. The masterminds, those who seek to reshape the world according to their vision, owe much of their success to a compliant media that parrots the same talking points across endless news cycles. While looking ridiculous and thoroughly undermining their credibility, parroting talking points reinforces prescribed narratives ad nauseum. This transformation of the media, from watchdogs of truth to mouthpieces for globalist power, has been stark and troubling.

In past eras, journalists held the powerful accountable, exposing corruption and safeguarding the underpinnings of a healthy republic. The media used to be watchdogs, bastions of truth, a voice for all citizenry, and especially the oppressed. But now, they have become modern-day house negroes tightly coordinated with the overlords' directives and manufactured narratives.

The field of journalism has transformed significantly. It evolved from a noble profession dedicated to safeguarding the interests of the public to become a tool of manipulation, often aligning with global elites and political powers. This shift has greatly contributed to the threats facing global society, and in many respects, has aided in the undermining of human flourishing of the general population. The media's involvement during worldwide crises, specifically the COVID-19 pandemic, prominence illustrates this. By overstating the severity of the virus and disregarding alternative treatments, the media failed to provide accurate information to the public, leading to unnecessary confusion, distrust, and loss of life. Instead of investigating the declining efficacy of vaccines or exploring potential alternative remedies such as ivermectin or hydroxychloroquine, journalists opted to vilify any form of skepticism. This biased and misleading reporting not only let down the public but also eroded societal trust, promoting a one-sided narrative that undermined public health that prolonged the pandemic.

Additionally, the media's handling of the pandemic and climate activism has prompted some journalists to question the validity of their profession. Journalists faced pressure to promote false narratives from influential entities that were beyond the realm of objective news reporting. Over the past decade, many journalists have openly challenged official media narratives and talking points. Those who dared to question the narratives imposed on them were subjected to derogatory remarks and criticism and ultimately dismissed from their careers.

The gross misinformation about the 2020 BLM/Antifa riots serves as a prime example of deceit and manipulation. Despite widespread looting, the deaths of officers, and the destruction of black and brown community businesses, the media fervently propagated the "mostly peaceful protests" narrative, ignoring the stark reality displayed on TV screens (businesses being burned in the background, gunshots being heard and mass-looting). Nevertheless, journalists adhered to contrived narratives and misinformation, disseminating blatant lies in the face of evident truth.

Journalism has shifted from a once noble profession aimed

at protecting the interests of the citizenry by reporting facts and truth to now an untrustworthy profession that receives its 'marching orders' and contrived narratives from overlords.

Furthermore, media narratives on climate change follow a similar trajectory, silencing dissenting scientific voices while amplifying hyperbolic narratives that align with global power interests. For instance, much of the climate research from the National Oceanic Atmospheric Association (NOAA) has been questioned as fraudulent; there is no consensus on climate change.[26] The culmination of events and associated directives has caused some journalists to question the very legitimacy of their profession. They feel pressured to promote false or exaggerated narratives dictated by powerful forces, which are far removed from the traditional roles of journalism. Journalists who dared to challenge these established narratives, such as Sharyl Attkisson, Glenn Beck, and Lara Logan, were often ostracized, surveilled, or driven out of their professions. These brave journalists have paid heavy personal and professional prices for their integrity, enduring threats, smear campaigns, and professional isolation. Their experiences testify to the high cost of journalistic integrity in today's media landscape.

MATTERS OF MEDIA... MATTERS!

Noam Chomsky and Edward Herman brilliantly illustrate how mass media serves the interests of elite groups by shaping

---

[26] Heartland Institute, "Climate Data Corrupted"- https://heartland.org/opinion/media-advisory-96-of-us-climate-data-is-corrupted/

public opinion and filtering information in ways that align with corporate, governmental, and institutional power in their book, "Manufacturing Consent: The Political Economy of the Mass Media." The book distills our current plight with journalism/mass media as it states: "The media serve the interests of the powerful elites, transmitting their messages to the public and shaping perceptions in ways that are consistent with elite interests. This system works not through overt censorship, but by filtering information and framing issues in a way that aligns with the dominant power structures."[27] This book explores the scheme of manipulation and argues that mass media, rather than being an independent and objective watchdog, is now a tool to propagate the agendas of powerful institutions (and overlords generally), subtly shaping public opinion in their favor—diabolical manipulation in order to control the masses. Using journalists and media in this way is evil, and some journalists have decided to take a stand against the evil..

Shrill and hysterical media assertions about "peaceful protests" (in the midst of riots), "vaccines are safe and effective" (while they were untested and ineffective), "the border is completely secure" (while tens of millions cross over and invade), "Biden operates with vigor and vitality (while he experiences significant metal decline)," are just some of the parroted obvious media lies.

Endless cycles of these types of reprobation led Tucker

---

27 Herman, Edward S., and Noam Chomsky. *Manufacturing Consent: The Political Economy of the Mass Media.* Pantheon Books, 1988

Carlson to take a stand, rejecting the parroting of talking points at Fox News and leaving Fox. Sharyl Attkisson, an investigative reporter for CBS News, was attacked and surveilled (her and her family's computers) when she exposed media lies and deceptions about Benghazi and the Fast and Furious operation (during Obama Administration); she ultimately left CBS News. Glenn Beck was always committed to exposing global deceptions and ultimately left CNN and Fox News. Lara Logan, a journalist for CBS News and "60 Minutes," left mainstream media due to frustration with the suppression of accurate reporting and myriad practices undermining journalistic integrity. All these journalists left mainstream journalism and paid a heavy price. Their families have been mercilessly targeted, they've had their lives threatened, and they've endured abuse (verbally and otherwise) by the cabal of masterminds (working on behalf of global overlords) overseeing all media. Why? Again, from the perspective of overlords, everyone must "stay on the plantation" and embrace groupthink, or be marginalized and abused to the point of irrelevancy. Freethinking is a threat to the overlords because it portends an imminent escape from the plantation; it must be quashed.

Yet, these stridently independent and heroic journalists continue their vital work and commitment to keep the public informed about what's truly happening. Their individual and collective drive is representative of hearts zealously unencumbered and controlled by others. They have hearts and minds determined to be free. They possess the zeal and desire of Frederick Douglass, Harriet Tubman, and Malcolm X; they have explored the pathology of the field negro. They are undeterred in pursuing free speech and freedom (generally) and have become a force to be reckoned with. Others see their example and are gaining strength and courage to do the same. Due to a resurgence of free-thinking Americans, the landscape of American politics is not doomed to subjugation under the rulership of overlords; there are now many now gaining strength and fortitude to embrace the pathology of field negro. When this occurs freedom expands.

The emergence of podcasters and other networks of content creators provides an encouraging trend in helping to forestall corrosive global subjugation while encouraging the pursuit of unalienable freedom.

Indeed, the historical role of journalism—as watchdogs, providers of balanced, accurate information, and facilitators of public discourse—has ended. Media outlets, which once empowered citizens to form their own opinions, now shape the public's mind with carefully crafted propaganda. The truth is no longer the focus; instead, the media spreads illusions of freedom constructed by those who seek to dominate. The media (generally) is captured. Media and journalists have now become the pretorian guard of overlords. They are now a favored tool of globalists to help bring about globalist control.

Any sincere observation and analysis of this group would objectively confirm that this group is wholly gripped by the pathology of the house negro and, as the first priority, commits to the dictates of overlords.

THE POWER OF PROPAGANDA: OVERLORD OBAMA'S TACTICS OF MASS DECEPTION

Plainly stated, the media (generally) now represents a major segment of the house negro pathology as it persists in the modern age; they are obedient and eager to serve, rewarded with access, influence, and the illusion of power. But never truly in control. They are used as just another piece on the board, moved by unseen hands, As long as they obediently protect the interests of the overlords, the power of overlords will remain unchallenged. What changed the role of media and journalism in America? How and why have media and associated journalists become the primary tool of globalists' interests and propaganda? It can be precisely narrowed down to Barak Obama's modification of the Smith-Mundt Act.

The decline of media integrity is especially alarming in light of the Smith-Mundt Act. The Smith-Mundt Act of 1948, initially designed to promote U.S. government viewpoints abroad and counter foreign propaganda, was amended by President Obama in 2013 through the Smith-Mundt Modernization Act. This amendment lifted the domestic dissemination ban, allowing the U.S. government to engage in information campaigns within the United States. In the context of propagandizing to empower masterminds, the Act's modernization allows for government messaging to influence and manipulate public opinion domestically.[28] By enabling the dissemination of

---

[28] Source: Libertarian Institute, 2022- https://libertarianinstitute.org/articles/the-smith-mundt-moderniziation-act-from-propaganda-to-censorship-to-tyranny/

government-produced content within the U.S., propaganda is no longer frowned upon or criminalized. Instead, it provides a perfect pathway to shape public perception and consolidate control, effectively empowering those in positions of power to steer narratives and reinforce their influence. The point is that propaganda is now unabashedly used to drive cultural narratives and public sentiment. In the minds of Obama and his acolytes, propaganda is critical to ushering in the ability to "totally transform America." The power of propaganda is limitless, and Edward Bernays perfected it to be used as a tool of manipulation and control.

The "Father of Propaganda," Edward Bernays, was the nephew of Sigmund Freud, and he applied his uncle's theories of psychology to influence public opinion on a large scale. He is best known for his groundbreaking work in developing techniques of persuasion that shaped the modern advertising and public relations industries.

Bernays believed that the masses could and should be influenced and controlled by appealing to their subconscious desires and emotions. He coined the term "engineering of consent" to describe the process of manipulating public opinion to serve the interests of governments and corporations. In his 1928 book *Propaganda*, Edward Bernays outlined his ideas and techniques, arguing that propaganda was a necessary tool for managing democratic societies. However, it is crucial to acknowledge that propaganda, when designed and implemented with unethical or malicious intent, can ultimately contribute to the downfall of entire societies. In an article about

Bernays published in *Medium*, journalist Swati Suman writes, "While branding can positively influence, it also carries the risk of deceiving the masses. Advertising that lacks moral and ethical principles is likely to foster skepticism and, rather than uplifting humanity, may lead to its downfall."[29]

Nefarious governments have used Edward Bernays' propaganda techniques to manipulate public opinion, maintain power, and suppress dissent. By appealing to base emotions and crafting persuasive narratives, insidious regimes have fostered extreme societal divisions, justified authoritarian actions, and controlled opposition. Propaganda shapes ideological narratives, diverts blame during crises, legitimizes surveillance and repression, and exploits modern media and technology to reinforce government-approved narratives. Through these methods, governments have effectively engineered consent, manipulating populations to align with their agendas and sustain their control. This is the tool Obama unleashed and the media and journalists employ (generally) to assuage the dictates of global overlords.

As long as the media remains in lockstep with the masterminds, the power of the overlords will go unchallenged. The once-proud role of journalism has regressed into a focus on propaganda, abandoning the truth and instead feeding the public narratives designed to maintain control. Without a great awakening of the American public, the supranational sovereignty of an intellectual elite and world bankers will remain

---

[29] https://swati-suman.medium.com/how-edward-bernays-manipulation-through-propaganda-became-marketing-history-d916cafa928d

inevitable, with the media standing as the obedient servants of their agenda. As long as they believe they are part of the masterminds/elites, they will project and protect the dictates of the elites.

Based on Obama's edicts, reinforced through the Smith-Mundt Act of 2012, we observe outright lies and deceit being reported as absolute truth from the pretorian media; their complicity in embracing the house negro pathology is manifest! The media mob is demonstrably unrelenting.

THE RISE OF INDEPENDENT VOICES: PIONEERING PODCASTERS

With record levels of media malpractice and malfeasance, podcasters are an emerging new force in journalism. This segment helps disseminate more accurate, truthful information without being filtered through overlord talking points. With the use of "nonsanctioned" (not parroted and contrived reporting) journalistic talking points and sources, truth can be more readily conveyed. I believe this segment is responsible for ultimately ending the COVID-19 vaccine and mask mandates. These journalists helped save lives (via truth about Ivermectin and other remedies). The podcast journalist/content creator segment is growing because citizens are realizing there is too much actual news being manipulated and underreported via traditional news sources. Social Media platforms host excellent prognosticators who provide insight and exposition. I follow a mix of podcasters and news sources, all of whom are free-thinking, independent, fearless, unrelenting, and faithful in the pursuit of freedom. Nothing But The News/James BCP, Glenn Loury, Jordan Peterson, Larry Elder, Vince Everett Ellison, Seth Gruber, April Chapman, Russell Brand, Melanie King, Isaiah Robin, David Harris Jr., Dan Ball/OAN, Mel K, and Patrick Byrne are just some of the people whom I find stridently and zealously advancing the field negroes desire for freedom powered by resistance to overlords. These are our modern-day heroes! They should be highly respected and admired for their commitment to truth and desire to remain vigilant, independent, and free, refusing to be ruled!

Challenges persist for individuals who value independent thinking and freedom. Their voices are being throttled and censored (and therefore their true reach is limited) via social media platforms. Globalist oligarchs understand that free speech fosters independent thought that can undermine their control. Social media platforms make it possible for dissenters, whistleblowers, and everyday people to give their information and views. Major global influences saw the widespread unfettered communication happening billions of times daily and decided not to allow the broad open communications. Instead, they have exerted significant control over these platforms, stifling the free exchange of ideas. For example, Zuckerberg and Facebook/Meta recently admitted to Congress that they have actively participated in suppressing free speech and moderating content that deviated from approved global narratives, including those related to COVID-19 and vaccines.[30] These ac-

---

[30] Zuckerberg Admission to Congress- https://abcnews.go.com/Technology/unpacking-mark-zuckerbergs-letter-congress-biden-facebook/story?id=113212652

tions, admitted to have been done at the behest of the Biden Administration and associated three-letter agencies, globally impacted and restricted free speech.

With the growth of social media over the past decade, it's clear that global influences have played major roles in censoring and limiting First Amendment rights to freedom of speech and publication in America. This is not just an American issue, however. All countries are now being forced to impose limits on speech. Brazil recently banned the X platform (formerly Twitter) due to its lack of censorship of speech and expression.[31] Google/YouTube is another info control player. Google has been implicated in active interference with elections over 41 times in the past 16 years.[32] The point is that all major social media platforms have been infiltrated and taken over by globalist ambitions to control mass populations. As globalist overlords monopolize and control social media, it becomes easier and more aggressive for them to push unfettered propaganda. These moves and methods all follow as part of the overlord syndrome.

Despite the systematic constraints, fiercely independent podcasters and content creators continue to champion free speech. Facing censorship, de-platforming, and demonetization, these individuals remain undeterred, driven by a deep commitment to truth. Their voices are instrumental in shaping and

---

[31] X banned in Brazil- https://www.bbc.com/news/articles/crkmpe53l6jo

[32] Google Interference- https://www.msn.com/en-us/news/politics/google-has-interfered-with-elections-41-times-over-the-last-16-years-media-research-center-says/ar-BB1k4YY1

preserving global republics, embodying the boldness of those who refuse to compromise their God-given right to freedom of expression. The spirit of Frederick Douglass, Harriet Tubman, and Malcolm X thrives via their embrace of the part rebellious, part freedom-seeking mind and soul of the field negro.

Other major segments and domains of society cry out for true liberation. Just as podcasters are ushering in vital reformations in the domain of journalism and media, the domain of region and Faith must also undergo reformation in order to parishioners to truly experience God, and to be set free.

PASTOR/MINISTER MOBS: THE EMBRACE OF GODLESS GLOBALIST "GOSPELS"

There are numerous examples of how global elites exert undue control over society. Though relatively few in number, they rely heavily on propaganda, deceit, and a vast network of complicit individuals to maintain power. Overlords prey on weak individuals who demonstrate an embrace of the house negro pathology. They are given gratuitous compensation and influence, or pressured into compliance (obedience) to the dictates of overlords. In return, these emasculated minions help the overlords seize control of nearly every sphere of society, including Faith-full spaces like churches. Even sacred domains, like the domain of Faith, can relatively easily be captured and many fundamentals of Faith are "turned on their heads" due to diabolical schemes designed to weaken Biblical authority in deference to the whims of secular culture. From the overlords' perspective, the significance of Christ (His birth, sacrifice, and victory) and Biblical authority be "damned"; all church leaders must submit to the new order. The overlords openly demonstrated their mindset during the Covid-19 period, locking down churches and forbidding religious meetings. When it comes to the act of bowing in submission, overlords demand the bowing be done at the "alter" of secular authority, not divine authority (God).

Disturbingly, the infiltration of faith institutions by insidious forces has profoundly weakened biblical authority in favor of secular, worldly whims. The domain of religion—once staunch in its opposition to world systems—has now become compromised. For example, Christians historically stood firmly for God's definition of marriage (one man and one woman in divine unity) and human life (a God-ordained creation that He is so particular about that He counts the hairs on each head), opposing redefinitions and abortion. Today, however, many pastors and churches have accommodated cultural pressures that wholly conflict with biblical truth. Dereliction and reprobation rampage in the church (generally).

People of faith have consistently been against shedding innocent blood by taking innocent life in the womb, and therefore wholly against abortion. They are also aware that, in the beginning (in the Garden of Eden), God created two biological species consisting of male and female, possessing XY and XX chromosomes, respectively. However, globalist schemes to undermine faith foundations and thus to escalate depopulation, tactics motivated by Karl Marx and Marxism, have taken root. Pastors and ministry leaders are now often just giving in to syncretize and accommodate emerging cultural trends. Biblical foundations confirming God's principles and designs for humanity are no longer "non-negotiables." For the most part, the powerful trends are not resisted but instead accepted.

This cultural infiltration is broad, impacting myriad issues, including pandemic responses. When COVID-19 struck, many churches closed, disregarding biblical admonitions to "not forsake the assembly." Even now, some congregations have not recovered to their pre-pandemic attendance levels. Churches that surrendered most have typically paid a price.

Cultural divides, fueled by ideologies like Critical Race Theory (CRT) and Diversity, Equity, and Inclusion (DEI), have also created fissures in church unity, thus cracking a concept central to the New Testament's teachings. The Cross once served as the unifying factor, transcending race, ethnicity, and gender. Today, however, cultural divisions are given precedence, and biblical oneness is abandoned in favor of divisive secular ideologies. Instead of upholding the purity of the Gospel message that establishes there are no barriers (between male/female, Jew/gentile, etc.) in Ephesians 2:14-20 and Galatians 3:25-26, many have abandoned oneness within the body of Christ as the only acceptable standard. Unity can only be rooted in this truth, so as the church abandons this vital truth, race divisions rooted in themes permeating a demon-infused culture become permanent. Deference to culture instead of reliance on the Cross is an abomination. It says what Christ did on the Cross was insufficient to address our current social and political paradigms. This is an anathema bred from overlords and readily imbibed by some of the largest ministries in America. We see again the pathology of house negroes in this movement toward performing as dupes for demonic overlords.

An example of this surrender to cultural forces appears in many notable pastors. Creflo Dollar, for instance, endorsed and promoted Stacey Abrams, as "the next Governor of Georgia." Abrams is a politician who is openly pro-abortion, pro-LGBT, and aligned with Marxist ideologies—positions that stand in direct opposition to biblical values.[33] The people of Georgia should be ecstatic Dollar's audacious proclamation did not materialize. The actions of Creflo Dollar demonstrate he is smitten by the house negro pathology.

Creflo is not alone in bending to the whims of culture (and demonism therein). TD Jakes also took a dark turn by gleefully announcing and commending Beto O'Rourke to his church during a recent election. Beto O'Rourke is a politician known for his anti-Christian stances.[34] Beto is known also for touting ideologies that subvert the entire Bill of Rights (especially the First and Second Amendments). By lauding Beto, Jakes "goosestepped" on behalf of the overloads by ignoring the significance of the Word of God and the necessity to overlay the Kingdom/Gospel onto all domains (especially political/civic engagement) as the way forward to Christians committed to

---

[33] Creflo Dollar applauds Abrams- https://charismanews.com/opinion/what-does-his-endorsement-of-stacey-abrams-stay-about-this-well-known-pentecostal-pastor/

[34] Jakes lauds Beto- https://www.yahoo.com/news/beto-orourke-visits-t-d-143013175.html

living and voting Biblically. Instead, he demonstrated profound deference to what are likely his familial political and voting traditions, as well as to the whims of cultural pressures. Such conduct exemplifies the pathology associated with the 'house negro' mindset.

These actions by church leaders reveal a troubling deference to secular culture and political correctness over biblical truth. These actions are driven by the pathology of the house negro. Why have pastors acquiesced? The house negro pathology nullifies faith foundations, morals, personal principles, and logic. Overlords promote the pathology to build its power for control.

It's alarming how cultural capitulation has permeated the faith community so deeply. Once held accountable for adhering to the word of God, many faith leaders now succumb to worldly pressures, undermining the integrity of the church itself. This abandonment of the Cross, and the Word, for the whims of culture, is not only tragic but also a stark betrayal of the Gospel. The house negro pathology, fueled by cultural compensation and influence, has metastasized into the church, leading to a surrender of faith at the altar of secular overlords.

In her newly released book, Megan Basham's *Shepherds for Sale*, helps confirm the current plight of the church. The book states, "The Christian leaders who once stood as beacons of moral clarity are now, in many cases, little more than mouthpieces for worldly powers and cultural trends." This is sad and pathetic but very true. Basham's book confirms how progressive powerbrokers have infiltrated evangelical churches, targeting institutions like Christian media, universities, and megachurches. Basham highlights specific pastors who have compromised biblical teachings in exchange for political influence or financial gain. Left-wing billionaires, including George Soros, have strategically co-opted religious leaders to push progressive agendas, especially on issues like sexuality, abortion, and systemic racism.

Shepherds for Sale highlights various ways influential pastors align themselves with progressive or unbiblical ideologies under the guise of social justice and racial reconciliation. Specifically naming the late and very influential pastor, Tim Keller, the book scrutinizes his adopting leftist-progressive views, particularly concerning issues like poverty and social justice. Consider Keller's famous quote: *"If you see people who are poor and you see people who are in trouble, if you don't love them, you aren't loving God. You aren't loving your neighbor. You aren't loving your neighbor as yourself."* The surface-level appeal of Keller's statement hides a deeper alignment with progressive political policies. Considering the state of the most innocent among us, human life in the womb, a principled Keller would have mentioned the most basic demonstration of this "love your neighbor" commitment is the unequivocal commitment to protect life in the womb.

Consider, too: A principled and biblical Keller would confirm that open borders tacitly encourage the worst human rights atrocities on the planet at the moment (child rapes, sex trafficking, human trafficking) and therefore our love for them compels getting rid of the inducement (by putting up more walls/barriers) for them to come here vulnerable and unprotected to be enslaved by cartels and traffickers. You can't assert you "love" people and then encourage them to risk their life (many are killed making the trek), dignity (far too many are horribly raped multiple times on the way here, sex/human trafficking when they arrive), and liberty (too many are perpetually enslaved after they arrive). Keller demonstrates a full embrace of the house negro pathology as he allows his political alignment and allegiance to dictate his actions (as opposed to the Word of God). The overload/globalists delight in Tim Keller as he gives credence to their agendas.

Another key figure Basham helps us understand is Russell Moore, former head of the Ethics & Religious Liberty Commission of the Southern Baptist Convention. Like the derelictions of Keller, Moore promotes leftist Progressive views on immigration and race. Basham asserts people like Moore have allowed political and social pressures to influence their theology, aligning themselves with movements that diverge from traditional Christian teachings on morality, sexuality, and the sanctity of life. Moore appears guilted and ashamed of the Gospel as he gives wide deference to cultural tropes about racism. Moore's departure from the Gospel is a cause for disappointment, as he should be standing on the Gospel and the finished works of the Cross, instead of giving platitudes and empty, pathetic commitment to "do better."

Basham confirms that other well-known Christian leaders, including Rick Warren, David Platt, Ed Stetzer, and J.D. Greear, consistently blur the lines between biblical teachings and political activism. Each of these pastors embraces an approach to Christendom intended on "balancing faith" with social issues; this inevitably leads to progressive Christianity. An anathema!! There is little doubt these men are captured by the secular globalist agenda. They willfully closed their respective churches and participated in the global pandemic funding provided to individuals and institutions who cooperated with tactics designed to undermine Faith institutions. For some, compensation is a strong motivator. They surrender faith convictions (that include fellowship of the saints) and the Gospel message (sufficiency of the finished works of the Cross, "one in Christ" and unity), in deference to dictates from antichrist overlords when enough compensation from the global overlords is forthcoming. With current levels of malfeasance, dereliction, and reprobation in American pulpits, Basham's book is right on target.

SANGERS' "NEGRO PROJECT": THE CHURCH UNDER SIEGE

Margaret Sanger was the founder of Planned Parenthood. Sanger is likely to have not heard of Malcolm X's characterizations of the house negro, but she was keenly perceptive of tactics of manipulation. She was both cunning and manipulative in advancing her insidiously racist ideologies, particularly through her influence on church leaders. She sought not only to undermine black communities but also to weaken Christian orthodoxy, crafting calculated schemes to achieve both.

Sanger was deeply influenced by Darwinist principles and

advocated for eugenics, promoting the idea that reproduction should be encouraged among those with "desirable" traits while discouraged among those she deemed "undesirable." This ideology, rooted in selective breeding, reflected her belief in racial hierarchies. In essence, she viewed certain groups, particularly black people, as inferior and unequal in dignity and worth. As an atheist and eugenicist, Sanger's beliefs aligned with the tenets of White supremacy. Like Darwin, she supported racial hierarchies, viewing black people as "subhuman."[35]

Motivated by the eugenics movement, Margaret Sanger devised calculated schemes to reduce birth rates among black populations, believing this would create a stronger, more "refined" society. To her, black people were a "stain" on humanity—tainted and unworthy in her view. It was from this deeply ingrained prejudice that she launched her so-called "clinics," which she envisioned as tools for the mass "extermination of the Negro population"—her own chilling words.

Sanger's disdain for black people was unmistakable. She did not hide it, often aligning herself with the Ku Klux Klan, speaking at their women's events and finding common ground in her shared vision of racial purity. Beneath the guise of public health and reproductive rights, she harbored a venomous hatred for black people, a hatred that drove her to mask her real intentions with cunning.

---

[35] Sanger Racist Eugenicist- https://womanisrational.uchicago.edu/2022/09/21/margaret-sanger-the-duality-of-a-ambitious-feminist-and-racist-eugenicist/

She concocted a plan to deceive the very people she sought to eliminate. This plan, which she proudly dubbed "The Negro Project," was designed to accelerate what she hoped would be the self-destruction of the black population. It was a masterful manipulation, cloaked in the language of empowerment but grounded in the ugliest form of racial animosity. Sanger, a virulent white supremacist, had one clear objective: to further her vision of a world rid of those she deemed inferior.

ABORTION: A TOOL OF WHITE SUPREMACY

Margaret Sanger saw herself as part of an elite class, superior to others, and committed to the depopulation of those she deemed undesirable. Embracing a mindset reminiscent of an overlord, Sanger initiated what would become a controversial plan in 1939: the Negro Project. This initiative was designed to significantly reduce the black population with the help, encouragement and support of black pastors. Sanger infamously stated, "We do not want word to go out that we want to exterminate the Negro population, and the minister is the man who can straighten out that idea if it ever occurs to any of their more rebellious members."[36] To ensure the cooperation of black pastors, Sanger emasculated and manipulated them with financial compensation, using their influence to advance her insidious agenda. This echoes the dynamic of the house negro pathology, employing manipulation and the promise of money and status to control

---

[36] Sanger Letter to Gamble-https://genius.com/Margaret-sanger-letter-from-margaret-sanger-to-dr-cj-gamble-annotated

and co-opt leadership. The use of money and power as tools of influence continues to be at the heart of the project's legacy, driving its foundations and maintaining its roots even today.

The Sanger Negro Project involved significant manipulation of black pastors by offering $100 for each sermon that advocated for and praised the "benefits" of abortion. This payment scheme mirrors the tactics used by oppressive systems to control and manipulate. The Spirit of the Lord does not guide pastors who accept such payments rather they are unduly influenced by a "Judas spirit."

The "Judas spirit" represents betrayal, deception, and self-interest; it manifests in situations where loyalty is expected, but hidden treachery is present. Judas Iscariot, a disciple of Jesus, exemplifies this when he betrays Jesus despite having shared in His ministry and teachings. In the church, this spirit is evident when pastors or ministers compromise their principles for money or power. Margaret Sanger's Negro Project is a stark example of the Judas spirit in action.

To this day, many black pastors continue to bow to the pressures of cultural trends and the agendas of depopulation advocates, unknowingly adhering to the foundations of the Negro Project. Rather than feeling shame for promoting evils like abortion and supporting racism and white supremacy—concepts deeply rooted in the KKK's ideology—they project these very accusations onto others who oppose the destructive practice of abortion. Are they truly unaware? How can they remain so willfully blind? The answer is simple: they are still being compensated.

While they may not receive direct payment for each sermon today, they gain compensation in the form of "social cred," societal acceptance, and preferred positions within progressive political parties. These faith leaders, in advocating for abortion on behalf of depopulationist overlords, are actively endorsing schemes steeped in racism and white supremacy. These practices are designed to promote Black genocide, as the disproportionate targeting of black communities leads to a disproportionate number of black babies being lost.

The point is that the house negro syndrome is alive and well within the church, largely due to the deceptions and manipulations stemming from Sanger's Negro Project. This project, driven by the racist and white supremacist designs of Margaret Sanger, exploited pastors by activating what can be called the "Judas spirit"—an ancient pathology that compels individuals to sell their souls for financial gain. Through this spirit, pastors and ministers were encouraged to abandon Biblical truth in favor of serving depopulationist agendas. Sadly, many pastors have fallen prey to these schemes, manipulated by the legacy of Sanger and the influence of globalist, racist elites.

Pastors supporting racism and supremacy while waxing hysterically about racism and supremacy? To any rational mind, this seems nonsensical. But through the lens of the house negro syndrome, it makes perfect sense—they have been captured.

There are numerous examples of pastors and ministers who have become manifestly derelict and reprobate, operating under the pathology of the house negro syndrome. Due to the pervasive blending of culture and faith, we can easily identify thousands of pastors, ministers and "Christian artists" who have been captured. Among the most notorious examples are Jamal Bryant (promoting marijuana use and sexual immorality), Andy Stanley (forming unholy alliances with LGBTQ trends), William Murphy (heavily syncretizing with demonic culture), father Pfleger (unholy alliances with cultural trends), Jiim Wallis (reprobate and derelict by subverting the Gospel in deference to culture), Dwight McKissic (inordinate focus on "race" and retribution, over the loving Gospel and act of forgiveness), COGIC Bishop John Sheard (decadent embrace of secular culture), the entire Conference of National Black Churches (CNBC), Lecrae, and the entirety of Evangelicals for Harris. These are just a few of the many who have demonstrated a consistent incongruence with the Word of God, bowing to a culture dominated by manifest demonism. Christians (and especially its leadership) are called to have "enmity with the world"—to resist and reject the world's systems and its culture. Yet these leaders capitulate, seeking to appease the very forces they should oppose. Instead of standing firm, they adopt worldly proclamations on sexual immorality, LGBTQ issues, the manipulation and defilement of children, and the acceptance of abortion and infanticide. Through their actions and intent, they have become enemies of God. James 4:4 reminds us: *"Do you not know that friendship with the world is enmity with God? Whoever therefore wants to be a friend of the world makes himself an enemy of God."* It should be manifest, the embrace of the house negro syndrome encourages separation from God and alignment with enemies of God.

We can be confident that there remains a faithful remnant of church leaders who have not bowed to the dictates of postmodern overlords. God has always preserved a remnant. Across America, there are pastors and ministers who stand firmly on God's Word, refusing to be bought or bargained with. For them, the Word is sacred and wholly sufficient, and the finished work of the Cross is "more than enough." They will not compromise or yield to cultural pressures, and they remain fearless in the face of society's corrosive demands.

Pastors and ministers like Jurgen Matthesius, Jack Hibbs, Bishop Patrick Wooden, David L. Lowery, Dennis Peacocke, Tommy E. Quick, Terrell Murphy, Voddie Baucham, Leon Benjamin, Alton Williams, Allen Jackson, John Amanchukwu, and Lucas Miles are just a few examples of great men of valor who unapologetically and uncompromisingly and consistently stand for God and the fullness of His Word. Based on their "fruits," it is clear that they are true bondservants of Christ, committed to remaining free from all coercion or bondage of any world system. They wholly reject coercion from culture or globalist overlords. These leaders exemplify not only Christlikeness but also hold the uncompromising and unwavering spirit and pathology of the field negro, free-thinking and against coercively cultural tides, standing firm in their faith and conviction while leading others to do the same (making disciples). These are modern-day heroes of Faith!

While God has raised great men to do great work in taking a stand against rampaging evils in these times, demonism is always lurking. And, it has now been embraced by large swaths of the church by way of neo-Marxism.

MARXISM IN THE CHURCH: FUEL FOR OVERLORD CONTROL

Many church leaders, swayed by cultural trends and pressured into complete obedience to the dictates of overlords, have become vulnerable to the notion that the Bible and the Gospel of Jesus are insufficient. They are encouraged to believe that "social activism" is the missing element that provides a more "complete" salvation, suggesting that the works of Jesus were somehow incomplete or lacking. This mindset has led many church leaders to embrace what the Apostle Paul warned about in Galatians 1:8-9—"another gospel." Ultimately, this opened the door for Marxist theologies to infiltrate the church, distorting and undermining the purity of the Gospel. This corruption gave rise to what is now known as Liberation Theology.

In the 1960s, many churches began to adopt Liberation Theology and Black Liberation Theology in response to perceived racial injustices, feeling that the Bible (and Christianity in general) did not sufficiently address these issues. Liberation Theology finds its roots in South American Marxism, emerging in Latin America with the belief that the Church's primary role is to combat poverty and inequality rather than disciple people in the Gospel of the Kingdom. This theology emphasizes that God aligns with the oppressed and calls for resistance against unjust societal structures. Black Liberation Theology, developed by James Cone during the Civil Rights and Black Power movements, focuses specifically on racism and interprets Christ's message as one of liberation from oppression. These movements blended faith with activism, leading churches to replace the Bible's affirmation of Biblical justice—affirmed throughout scripture—with the neo-Marxist concepts of "social justice" and "black liberation."

James Cone, the pioneer of Black Liberation Theology, believed that the Bible alone was insufficient in addressing the struggles of Black people. He asserted, "One of the tasks of Black theology is to analyze the nature of the Gospel of Jesus Christ in light of the experience of oppressed Blacks." For Cone, no theology could be considered truly Christian unless it arose from the oppressed and interpreted Jesus' work as fundamentally about liberation. In his view, Christian theology must be understood through the lens of systemic and structural relationships, primarily between two groups: the oppressed (victims) and the oppressors (victimizers).[37] [38] Needless to say, these structures are the fundamental elements of Marxism (i.e. bourgeoisie vs. proletariat). This is how Marxism has infiltrated and began to be rooted in psyche of Faith/religion.

It is ironic that many in the church embrace Karl Marx's ideologies, given his openly loathsome antichrist stances. Marx was a staunch atheist who harbored a deep hatred for any notion of God. He was wholly driven by a desire to "dethrone God" wherever He existed. In one of his diatribes, Marx expressed his disdain for God and his inclination toward hell, writing, "Thus heaven I've forfeited, I know it full well. My soul,

---

[37] https://www.acton.org/pub/commentary/2008/04/02/marxist-roots-black-liberation-theology

[38] Black Liberation Theology- Ezra Institute, June 2020 https://www.ezrainstitute.com/what-is-black-liberation-theology/

once true to God, is chosen for hell."[39] By definition, Karl Marx was a demonic fool.

Psalm 14:1 says, "The fool hath said in his heart, There is no God." We've already established that demonic forces influenced Marx, and now, by biblical definition, we can confirm that Marx was a fool. The same spirit of demonic foolishness is rampant in the church today through the spread of Liberation Theology and Black Liberation Theology. Despite their titles, those who advocate for these distorted theologies are, by biblical standards, also demonic fools.

With the embrace of Margret Sanger's schemes via the Negro Project and Karl Marx's ideologies designed to "dethrone God," we can see the house negro pathology spreads easily through pulpits infected with this demonic foolishness. This is especially harmful to parishioners, as these antithetical "other gospels" threaten the well-being of their souls. Galatians 1:8-9 warns, "But though we, or an angel from heaven, preach any other gospel unto you than that which we have preached unto you, let him be accursed. As we said before, so say I now again, if any man preach any other gospel unto you than that ye have received, let him be accursed." The Apostle Paul emphasized twice that deviations from the pure Gospel of Christ bring curses. Parishioners who sit under church leaders preaching messages syncretized with demonic culture, or infused with Liberation and Black Liberation theologies, are effectively

---

[39] Karl Marx Transcript- https://worldviewtube.com/worldviewpedia/transcript/karl-marx-1818-1883-and-his-stated-desire-dethrone-god-and-destroy

cursing themselves—and those vulnerable to these teachings. In such environments, the house negro pathology thrives.

The house negro pathology manifests in various ways throughout Christendom; it undermines Faith and is an existential threat to the soul. The remedy to this scourge and assault on Christendom is to wholly embrace the Word of God and the sufficiency monof finished works of the Cross; this requires free-thinking independence. An embrace of the pathology of the field negro is especially helpful here. It is the embrace of the field negro mindset that helps stand against and reject corrosive cultural trends, and through strict reliance on the Spirit of God, provide clarity of the Gospel message.

Those who adopt the psyche and pathology of the field negro are the ones who remain clear-eyed and principled, discerning Biblical truth with enlightened hearts. They can stand as vigilant "watchmen on the wall," praying for the veil to be lifted from the eyes of those blinded by culture and relentlessly pressured by globalist overlords.

Like Frederick Douglass, Harriet Tubman and Sojourner Truth who relied solely on God for their strength, freedom, and victory, embracing the mindset of the field negro enables us to reject false gospels and rest in the sufficiency of God's Word and the finished work of the Cross.

Five

Pathologies at Play in Today's America

WHO EMBRACES THE PATHOLOGY OF OVERLORDS AND HOUSE NEGROES?

With unveiled eyes, we should now be able to clearly distinguish between the house negro, overlord, and field negro pathologies that Malcolm X famously discussed. These were not casual or mean-spirited characterizations but rather prescient observations based on the experiences of historical heroes like Frederick Douglass, Sojourner Truth, and Harriet Tubman. These archetypes are deeply embedded in the American political landscape, influencing motivations, actions and intentions. The question remains: "Which one are you?"

Before answering this, we must confront some inconvenient truths about ourselves that we may not want to admit. Moving forward requires an honest baseline assessment. Lying to oneself is both destructive and counterproductive; clarity is essential for progress, power, and purpose. As Jordan Peterson explains, "If you practice violating your own conscience with a performative contradiction—a willingness to act out what runs contrary to your own sense of morality—then you become the embodiment of a lie... The danger of being an actor is that you become the actor, and in doing so, you lose yourself. You replace yourself with that falsehood, and that leads to bitterness, which can spiral into vengeance—and worse."

Peterson's statement is profound in that it challenges us to genuinely observe and confront our inherent tendencies. Those who find their general outlook and psyche constantly preoccupied with others' opinions and who are heavily shaped by cultural influences align with the house negro pathology. In contrast, those who are defiantly independent have an unrelenting commitment to unencumbered freedom and freethinking, and are unconcerned with societal trends or cultural mandates aligned with the field negro pathology. Meanwhile, individuals surrounded by wealth and power, who wield global influence and contribute significantly to shaping world economies, are considered as overlords.

Revealing these characterizations as pervasive archetypes helps to clarify actions and intentions. By understanding the pathologies that individuals or groups follow, we gain insight into our own behaviors and those of others. Media and entertainment, politics, religion/faith, and education are among the major spheres affected by these archetypes. Identifying prominent figures or organizations within these areas can further illuminate where we stand in relation to them, providing greater clarity. The purpose of this book is to offer a clearer understanding of the archetypes and pathologies that dominate the actions and intentions of significant influencers in our lives so that (if we deem it necessary) we can maneuver and change direction.

PATHOLOGY "GONE WILD" IN MEDIA/ENTERTAINMENT

One of the most dominant and influential domains shaping American politics is Media and Entertainment. Major media outlets such as CNN, MSNBC, ABC, NBC, Time Magazine, Politico, The New York Times, The Washington Post, BuzzFeed, Vox, the Los Angeles Times, and Newsweek, among others, are significantly influenced by globalist interests. These outlets uniformly provide parroted talking points under the guise of "news" that aligns with the agendas of those seeking to undermine free speech and individual freedoms.

For instance, these media organizations uniformly castigated and condemned anyone who questioned vaccines and related mandates. Instead of conducting thorough investigations into the origins and nature of the virus, or questioning the immense financial gains (estimated in the trillions) of global beneficiaries, they suppressed dissenting views. This one example (vaccines and viruses) demonstrates a lack of critical inquiry, and the adherence to a singular narrative highlights the extent of media control and its impact on public discourse. Today, there are very few who embrace the principles and ethics of "journalistic integrity."

By definition, mainstream media has largely been captured and are under the control of globalists, meaning it operates under the pathology of the house negro. Any sincere observer can easily discern that the actions and intentions of the mainstream media, with its level of obedient subservience to globalists, oligarchs, and powerful elites, confirm that this pathology dominates the domain.

Prominent journalists and podcasters who obediently conform to cultural demands and the dictates of these overlords, echoing the mainstream media's talking points, are included in the house negro archetype and pathology. Some of the most notable voices in this category include Mark Cuban, Roland Martin, Van Jones, Rickey Smiley, Stephen A. Smith, "Charlamagne tha god," Bill Maher, Howard Stern, Don Lemon, Kathy Griffin, Rosie O'Donnell Bette Midler, the entire cast of *The View*, Dana Bash, Barbra Streisand, Taylor Swift, Robert De Niro, Mark Zuckerberg, Joy Reid, Oprah Winfrey, Ben Stiller, and Jane Fonda, to name just a few of the shrill and hysterical voices, use their influence to consistently parrot dictates of overlords in order to help keep power and control over the masses. With notable levels of petulant adolescence, they deride all free-thinkers and castigate all who demonstrate any independence away from post-modern groupthink. These popular figures allow the demands of overlords and obedience to pathology to override basic logic, principles, human dignity, morals, and prudence. In this way, as they propagate lies and propaganda (not truth), their actions indicate alignment and close embrace with the pathology of house negro. They dutifully confirm they are enemies of freedom.

German historian and philosopher, Hannah Arendt, provides clarity as to why we are enduring perilous lying and propaganda from the media. She states, "This constant lying is not aimed at making the people believe a lie, but at ensuring that no one believes anything anymore. A people that can no longer distinguish between truth and lies cannot distinguish between right and wrong. And such a people, deprived of the power to think and judge, is, without knowing and willing it, completely subjected to the rule of lies. With such a people, you can do whatever you want." Arendt's powerful observation highlights the ultimate goal of the overlords: control and domination of the media as part of a calculated scheme to demoralize and subjugate the masses for their global ambitions. The house negro syndrome facilitates the erosion of freedom, allowing for the perpetual control and subjugation of those who have been captured by it. As noted, this syndrome has taken over major domains of communication, including media and entertainment, but its reach extends far beyond, influencing many other sectors as well.

A significant subset of entertainment is sports and athletics, which have also fallen under the heavy influence of the house negro syndrome. NBA superstars like Steph Curry and LeBron James, along with coaches like Gregg Popovich and Steve Kerr, and NBA legend Magic Johnson, are just a few prominent voices in sports whose actions seem to wholly comport with this syndrome. When Enes Kanter Freedom spoke out against modern-day slavery and abuses in China, he was met with universal disdain and dismissal from the NBA and its stars for standing by his principles and demanding justice for the enslaved. These figures (those conforming as NBA house negroes) often use social media to silence and shame those with dissenting views on government, economy, and culture, while eagerly promoting the dictates of their globalist overlords, heavily influenced and underwritten by the CCP. Without shame or remorse for their hypocrisy, however, they continue to pontificate about "justice" and "equity."

Ironically, justice and equity are not extended to those in media and entertainment who hold differing opinions or offer dissenting voices against the prevailing dictates of the overlords. Kevin and Sam Sorbo, Jon Voight, Ice Cube, James Woods, Dean Cain, Patrick Bet-David/Valuetainment, Dan Bongino, Steve Bannon, Dan Ball/OAN, Glenn Beck/Blaze, Tucker Carlson/TCN, Elon Musk, and John Solomon/Just The News are just a few who stridently stand against the collectivist orthodoxy in media and entertainment. They believe in and pursue freedom/free-thinking unvarnished truth, and are not swayed by the propaganda of brainwashed masses. All of them have paid a heavy price, and they and their families continue to bear a great burden for their stance, but they continue to stand unapologetically. To borrow from Malcolm X's characterizations, these individuals embody the pathology of the field negro, committed to free thinking and being set free from all encumbrances (especially cultural and political orthodoxy). They should be heralded as heroes; through their dedication to real justice and real equality for all (rejecting neo-Marxist "justice" and "equity" cliches), they consistently challenge the status quo with conviction.

When terms like "justice" and "equity" are used, they typically evoke an immediate emotional response. This is why they are often used as clichés to encourage alignment with postmodernist globalist ideologies. The domain where postmodernism thrives most is academia. Academic institutions, having bowed to the demands of global overlords, have also been captured and now serve as fertile breeding grounds for the house negro pathology.

EDUCATION SYSTEMS: BREEDING GROUNDS FOR OBEDIENCE, NOT EXCELLENCE

In the domain of education and academia, the house negro pathology runs rampant; it is pervasive. What were once institutions committed to learning, truth and meaning, have transformed into entities that teach vulnerable and malleable students how to march in lockstep with postmodern ideology obediently.

Historically, institutions of higher learning primarily served as centers of advanced education, research, and intellectual development. Their fundamental purpose was to cultivate critical thinking, provide specialized knowledge, and prepare individuals for professional careers. These institutions aimed to shape future leaders, promote civic responsibility, and advance societal progress through the dissemination of knowledge and innovation.

Now, these institutions have become caricatures of propaganda and Marxist revolution. They increasingly produce masses of obedient students willing to subserviently follow the dictates of globalist ideologies—often presented under the guise of "the greater good" or other forms of contrived utopian ideals. The result is an overwhelming number of students embodying the house negro pathology. How did this transformation occur? A significant factor is the influence of Project Paperclip.

Project Paperclip was a secret U.S. government program initiated after World War II to recruit German scientists, engineers, and technicians, who worked for the Nazi regime; they were Nazis![40] The program was supposed to leverage their expertise, especially in fields such as rocketry, aeronautics, and chemical weapons, in hopes of advancing American military might and technological capabilities during the early stages of the Cold War.

Despite many of these scientists' involvement in war crimes or their affiliations with the Nazi Party, the U.S. prioritized their skills, conveniently overlooking the moral concerns about their allegiance to Nazism. Over 1,600 German scientists were integrated into premier American academic institutions, research centers, military projects, and space exploration efforts.

These intellectuals eventually became involved in American academia and research institutions, influencing higher education and reshaping academic disciplines. This integration opened the door to a broader academic discourse, leading to the rise of new ideologies in U.S. universities, including Marxist thought.

---

[40] Annie Jacobson, *Operation Paperclip: The Secret Intelligence Program that Brought Nazi Scientists to America*, Little, Brown and Company, 2014.

Now, nearly 100 years later, with the incorporation of over 1,600 German intellectuals—many considered radical in their time—American universities are experiencing the rise of radical professors and students. Over time, the academic landscape in the U.S. saw a shift towards postmodern and critical theories, which are rooted in Marxist principles. This shift has been accompanied by an increasing presence of radical ideologies on college campuses. The traditional pursuit of objective truth and critical thinking has been replaced with a focus on social justice and equity, and contributing to a climate of ideological conformity. Radical revolutionaries embracing dreams of a post-modern utopia are now commonplace on college campuses. This is the fuel provided by cultural pressures that shape masses into stridently obedient individuals motivated to operate under the pathology of the house negro.

Due to the impact of Project Paperclip and the subsequent rampant proliferation and embrace of Marxist ideologies, Academia is wrought with radical revolutionaries. These revolutionaries have been manipulated into reflecting the anti-American sentiment of Project Paperclip academics and Karl Marx/Marxism.

Academia has become a cloistered cabal, with over 75% of its members identifying as Leftist Progressives, who are closely aligned with Marxist principles.[41] With collectivist uniformity, col-

---

[41] America First Policy – https://americafirstpolicy.com/issues/research-report-reversing-the-woke-takeover-of-higher-education-strategies-to-dismantle-campus-dei

leges are no longer designed to help students explore and find truth and creativity, they have become institutions of Marxist propaganda and groupthink. Leftist dominance fosters an ideal environment for shaping malleable minds into Marxist radicals, turning academic institutions into a veritable petri dish for revolutionaries eager to follow the ever-shifting tides of cultural trends.

It is important to note that many tenured professors and notable scholars like Robin DiAngelo, Ibram X. Kendi, Angela Davis, Michael Eric Dyson and Kimberlé Crenshaw dominate the airwaves and bookshelves, waxing poetic while encouraging a shift towards postmodernism. The foundations of their ideologies are rooted in Marxism, and they fundamentally advocate for radical Marxist revolutionaries. Diversity, Equity, and Inclusion (DEI) and Critical Race Theory (CRT) are just a few of the neo-Marxist frameworks designed to erode American traditions and push towards a "global reset" (as seen in the agendas of the World Economic Forum and Klaus Schwab's "Great Reset"). These influential academics follow the dictates of global elites, aiding in the creation of cloistered college environments where masses of students are indoctrinated into collectivist, radical revolutionary ideals.

When dissenting voices arise on college campuses, they are often shouted down and silenced. This stifles the environment for genuine exchange of ideas, fostering only conformity. Demands for strict adherence to ideological conformity result in the opposite of healthy learning environments, producing instead hardened Marxist "drones" incapable of navigating real-world issues. These students find solace in collective action and group-think, reflecting academia's role (in general) as an incubator for those students to be indoctrinated into the pathology of the house negro syndrome.

The only safeguard preventing all college campuses from fully descending into the abyss of Marxism are thinkers and activists who stand with the conviction and resolve characteristic of the field negro pathology. Notable figures like Charlie Kirk/TPUSA, Shelby Steele, Candace Owens, Frank Turek, Officer Tatum (Brandon), Jordan Peterson, and Eric Metaxas stand unapologetically for truth, freedom, freedom of speech, and principled education—free from ideological indoctrination. These individuals refuse to bow to pressure or have their voices silenced. They stand in righteous indignation against Marxism and any other ideologies that seek to undermine human flourishing.

The impact of academia being overwhelmed with Marxist ideology has a profound impact on leaders who have graduated from institutions of higher education. Those who have the most profound effect on the daily lives of all Americans are those who operate in the domain of politics. Politics overlays and impacts every domain in all of society. Therefore, laws and policies ultimately enshrined by politicians are inescapable. If politicians have been indoctrinated via college collectivist actions underpinned by Marxism, free speech, free-thinking, and free societies are threatened and are at risk of collapsing. Human flourishing becomes an unattainable goal when political leaders are indoctrinated and obedient to globalist overlords. Politics permeates every aspect of society, and the laws and policies that stem from it are unavoidable. If politicians are influenced by collectivist actions in college, rooted in Marxism, the very foundations of free speech, free thinking, and free societies are endangered, potentially leading to their collapse.

POLITICAL TREACHERY: THE OVERLORD'S BEST TOOL

When examining global elites such as Bill Gates, Jeff Bezos, Klaus Schwab, Xi Jinping, and George Soros through the lens of an "overlord" pathology, their actions and intentions—particularly regarding population control and global governance—become more apparent. Individuals who embody this pathology typically possess significant resources (often within the billionaire class), immense influence (garnered from high global standing), and authority (frequently from political positions or institutional power). Coupled with these attributes is a clear desire to limit human flourishing by limiting personal freedoms, such as free speech, the right to bear arms, and other fundamental rights.

At the core of this pathology is the drive to dominate and control others. More broadly, the ideology that fuels these figures is often characterized by authoritarian and or totalitarian tendencies, which align with the principles Marxism. As Thomas Sowell has explained so often, that ideology assumes that its adherents are "the anointed," i.e., in all ways "better than everyone else."

The interests of globalists, oligarchs, corporate elites, and cabals—driven by a Marxist foundation—pose a significant threat to global freedom. These forces have gained prominence due to their influence over key institutions such as the media, entertainment, and academia, all of which have been co-opted to serve their agenda. When they dictate talking points to journalists, make demands of academic institutions, and collude among themselves to socially engineer a new world order (such as the "Great Reset" proposed by the World Economic Forum), they exhibit the characteristics and pathology of overlords. To accumulate global power, these overlords heavily compensate media, academic, and political figures through lavish trips to Davos, Bilderberg meetings, exclusive G7 and G20 summits, and other elite gatherings where they scheme and strategize for global control. While these meetings are invitation-only, they cut across political lines and include individuals with various interests. The pathology of the overlord transcends party politics, seeking to establish a pervasive and overarching influence over all who are willing to pursue a new global order.

Policymakers and elected officials are targeted by overlords to help bring their globalist aspirations into reality. Heavily influenced by significant compensation, access to power, or deeply shaped by their upbringing and education, these individuals act as obedient house negroes in alignment with the agendas of their globalist overlords. Those who dissent from globalist orthodoxy receive shrill hysterics from voices like Keith Olbermann, Hillary Clinton, Cenk Uygur, Don Lemon, Joe Scarborough, Bernie Sanders, Mitch McConnell, Mitt Romney, Raphael Warnock, Rashida Tlaib, Ilhan Omar, Alexandria Ocasio-Cortez (AOC), Elizabeth Warren, and others;

these are incentivized (either by compensation, "access", or seats of power), and therefore use their power and influence to push for conformity of the masses as the U.S. moves closer to globalist control. It is no surprise that those most aligned with the audacious vision of a global utopia are unified in their embrace of Marxism, Leftism, and or Progressivism or globalism. In America, the Democratic Party primarily serves as the vehicle for advancing the globalist agenda. This raises the question, "Can Democrats and/or Progressives be trusted with maintaining and securing our Constitutional Republic for future generations?" Malcolm X distrusted Democrats and provided valuable insight and "food for thought" when considering this question.

Malcolm X characterized the Democratic Party as following the manipulative tactics of overlords, continually deceiving black voters into supporting them without any real promises in return. On a micro level (within the U.S.), this characterization fits, but on a macro (global) scale, the Democratic Party is just another tool obediently following the dictates of globalist elites. In both cases, as Malcolm X pointed out, the party is diabolically deceitful, using black voters to gain power without addressing the daily struggles of black communities. He brilliantly stated, "Any time you throw your weight behind a political party that controls two-thirds of the government and that party can't keep the promise that it made to you during election time, and you're dumb enough to walk around continuing to identify yourself with that party, you're not only a chump but a traitor to your race."

Holding elected officials accountable is essential in a

democratically elected Constitutional Republic. When we fail to do so, we become political chumps and traitors. Collective groupthink in the march toward a Marxist global order not only betrays the commitment to freedom but produces legions of "traitors" who, like the house negro, obediently following the commands of their overlords.

Of all motivated minions who embrace the pathology of the house negro, the most dangerous is the strident Liberal, Leftist, and Progressive. This is the type of house negro who sees everyone and anyone as a "means to an end." Their focus is keeping overlords happy by adopting a firm grip on ideology, not principles for human flourishing. In a Malcolm X speech "Ballot or the Bullet," he states, "The white liberal is the worst enemy to America, and the worst enemy to the black man. Let me explain what I mean by the white liberal. In America, there is no such thing as a Democrat or a Republican anymore. In America, you have liberals and conservatives. The white liberals, who have posed as our friends, have been the ones who have pushed us into the civil rights struggle. And they've used us to get their legislation passed." Malcolm X's chagrin was that white liberals, while claiming to support black people, often acted out of self-interest or paternalism (what I call, "condescending cynical saviors") rather than genuine principled commitment to black flourishing. He saw them as much more deceitful than conservatives because they posed as friends, allies, and supporters but consistently failed to address the real needs and concerns of the black community.

DESPERATELY DELUDED DESPOTS OF THE DEMOCRAT PARTY

While Democrats aggressively push their policies, many are delusional in believing that the utopian visions of planned societies and economies, as dictated by globalist elites, are achievable. Most Democratic politicians are fully aware of the detrimental effects of these plans on human flourishing, yet they persist in advocating for them. With their advanced education, they are also aware of the racist origins of Margaret Sanger's agenda, particularly her promotion of black genocide through abortion and her connection to the KKK, yet they continue to champion Sanger's schemes to promote abortion. Their primary objective is to appease globalist elites, using their political power to advance depopulation efforts while ignoring the disproportionate harm inflicted on black communities. These politicians, aligned with globalist agendas, represent a profound betrayal of their own communities. They operate with the mindset of what Malcolm X referred to as house negroes.

Barack Obama, Kamala Harris, Jesse Jackson, Al Sharpton, Cornel West, Derrick Johnson, Jim Clyburn, Hakeem Jeffries, and the Congressional Black Caucus exemplify what Malcolm X described as house negroes—individuals who betray their communities for personal gain. They leverage their political affiliation (Democratic Party), race (black identity), and public appeal (charisma and personality) to secure positions of power while concealing their true intentions: obediently following the dictates of globalist elites. Rather than genuinely advocating for the empowerment of their communities, these leaders align with globalist agendas, advancing policies such as depopulation through abortion—an agenda rooted in racist ideologies advocating black genocide via unfettered abortions. Malcolm X also characterized despotic types as traitors to their race.

Those who stand for the flourishing of the black community, by contrast, are often ostracized, disparaged, and silenced by these house negro politicians working to fulfill the objectives of their globalist overlords. Thankfully, the voices of free thinkers like Ben Carson, Byron Donalds, Tim Scott, Donald Trump, Mark Robinson, and Alveda King (among many others)—who stridently oppose abortion—will not be silenced by threats or slander. They are committed to ensuring freedom for all, beginning with the fundamental right to life for all. The spirit of independence, and resistance, once championed by field negroes, is evident in these modern-day stalwarts of freedom.

IS AMERICA DOOMED WITH SO FEW VOICES OF FREEDOM?

Russian-born American writer and philosopher Ayn Rand offered profound insights into the fate of societies on the brink of collapse, particularly those that seem beyond recovery. Reflecting on the pervasive influence of insidious globalist elites over media, entertainment, education, and politics, one cannot help but feel the overwhelming and near-ubiquitous control they exert. This raises the sobering question: *Is America doomed?*

Ayn Rand was prescient in many ways, offering this poignant observation about the downfall of society: "When you see that trading is done, not by consent, but by compulsion—when you see that in order to produce, you need to obtain permission from men who produce nothing—when you see that money is flowing to those who deal, not in goods, but in favors—when you see that men get richer by graft and by pull than by work, and your laws don't protect you against them, but protect them against you—when you see corruption being rewarded and honesty becoming a self-sacrifice—you may know that your society is doomed."[42] This quote emphasizes the dire consequences that can arise when corruption is celebrated and rewarded, while honesty and integrity are disregarded or even punished. It suggests that when a society reaches a point where dishonesty is prevalent and honesty is seen as a sacrifice, it is a clear indication of its impending downfall. The quote serves as a warning, urging us to be vigilant and take action against corruption in order to safeguard the future of our society.

Many of Ayn Rand's predictions, once seemingly disconnected from reality, now reflect our current dystopian reality in America, as her ideas have become more prophetic. She masterfully understood the insidious nature of power in the hands of those with nefarious intentions. Her description provides a glimpse into the global dystopia we now endure, orchestrated by duplicitous global elites. In light of her quote on "a nation's doom," again, ask ourselves: "Are we doomed?"

---

[42] Top 10 Ayn Rand Quotes to Inspire Individualism and Objectivism https://www.blinkist.com/magazine/posts/ayn-rand-quotes-inspire-individualism?utm_source=cpp

After evaluating America through Malcolm X's archetypes (house negro, field negro, overlord) and Ayn Rand's insights, the question arises: "Has America reached a point of doom?" I argue that it has not. America is not doomed because the spirit of "inspired individualism and objectivism," as described by Ayn Rand, is evident. Additionally, the resilience characteristic of Malcolm X's field negro archetype is increasingly present. As more Americans adopt this determined resolve, we move closer to reigniting and ultimately achieving global freedom.

ANSWERING THE CALL: CHAMPIONING THE PATHOLOGY OF THE FIELD NEGRO

The answer to oppression and tyranny, whether on a literal plantation or a plantation of the mind, is escape. Escape is only possible through fortitude, resolve, and unwavering commitment. This is the psyche and pathology embraced by field negroes of the past and is reflective of those harnessing the pathology today.

Field negroes today may no longer endure whips, chains, or the threats of lynching like those of the past; fortunately, the era of chattel slavery in America is over. However, that doesn't mean the threats to life and liberty have vanished. The same pathologies and psyches that once drove people to oppress and strip away innate freedoms are still at play. Although more covert and subtle, the mindset that motivated plantation overlords—and the house negroes who supported their power—remains rampant. These syndromes have become pervasive, spreading across societies and cultures through the strategies of globalist policymakers and legislators. The only way to resist and overcome them is through the embrace of the same determined spirit that once drove people toward freedom: the unyielding resolve of the field negro.

Being ostracized, subjected to the aggressive tactics of cancel culture (including doxxing), and facing threats to themselves and their families are results from the methods used today to silence and intimidate. However, those who embody the pathology of the field negro are neither restricted nor intimidated in their pursuit of freedom. They are driven by a genuine, righteous indignation rooted in their innate, God-given right to liberty.

Now is the time to stand up and reclaim freedom. With our resolve growing as we witness notable public figures leading the charge, we can forestall "doom" to the republic by also embracing an unwavering commitment to freedom. Several public figures come to mind who have faced threats and ridicule from globalist overlords and their obedient house negroes in media, entertainment, and politics, yet continue to press forward defiantly, embodying the unyielding spirit of Malcolm X's characterization of the field negro. These figures include Donald Trump, Tucker Carlson, Robert F. Kennedy, Jr., Glenn Beck, Glenn Greenwald, Dan Bongino, Chris Rufo, James O'Keefe, Elon Musk, Ben Bergquam, Jordan Peterson, James Lindsay, Russell Brand, Jason Whitlock, and Tulsi Gabbard. Alongside these individuals, a few media outlets come to mind that have resisted globalist pressures and the creeping influence of Marxism. The Washington Times, The Blaze, OAN, and

Epoch Times remain committed to hiring journalists who prioritize research and truth over coercion. These outlets, along with a growing number of others, are courageous and driven by an unwavering demand for freedom. All who remain strong and defiant driven by an insatiable need (demand) for freedom hold the keys to help restore the republic and foster liberty on a global scale. Like Frederick Douglass and other valiant heroes who have come before, these embody the spirit of honorable field negroes.

"Which One Are You"

INTROSPECTIVE PERSPECTIVE

America stands at another pivotal moment in its history, where the fight to restore and safeguard freedom is paramount. This battle demands individuals of unwavering resolve who are unafraid to confront genuine threats. For America to understand and navigate the current political landscape, it is essential to recognize the three fundamental pathologies shaping it. When people grasp the motivations behind these forces, they will be better equipped to make informed choices. This book uncovers the underlying dynamics and connects the dots between the various pathologies and motivations that drive individuals as they navigate the American political landscape. It should no longer be a mystery why so many suffer from Trump Derangement Syndrome (TDS) or why there is such contempt for free thinkers and conservatives who resist the march toward

Marxist globalism. We now see. We now discern. "We see them!"

We now understand how pseudo-intellectuals like Joy Reid, Whoopi Goldberg, Rachel Maddow, Joy Behar, and Bill Maher loudly and venomously express disdain for those with dissenting views. These individuals are not merely commentators—they are paid actors, deliberate propagandists, and "puppets on a string," performing for their overlords. Their tactics—shaming and derision—are tools to foster and maintain a culture of collective Leftist Progressive groupthink.

What we are witnessing in the domains of media and entertainment is nothing more than Kabuki theater, confirming how deeply these individuals have been manipulated by those who control them (globalist overlords). Now we can discern their motives; "We see them!" They are manifesting the pathology of the house negro, and they too need to be "set free." Rather than engage in endless arguments or name-calling, we should pray for these unfortunate souls who are trapped in an unrelenting pathology they don't even realize controls and enslaves them.

Politicians are suffering from a similar plight. This group of smooth-talking yet woefully misguided performers—including Obama, the Clintons, the Bushes, the Cheneys, and Kamala Harris—becomes insufferable to those who now recognize their misguided efforts to cede American sovereignty to Marxist globalist overlords. Aware that they are mere puppets answerable to a larger global agenda, we should pity them as they engage in desperate attempts to warmonger and fearmonger the American people; they've been "captured." Malcolm X's archetypes allow us to clearly discern why these figures are shrill, hysterical, and dismissive of the struggles of everyday Americans. They operate under the pathology of the house negro. "We see them!"

As we've uncovered, several individuals and organizations, entrenched in their respective pathologies, actively scheme to restrict American freedoms and hinder human flourishing globally. One of the most troubling and powerful sectors bowing to secular culture and the demands of global overlords, rather than bowing to God, is the realm of faith and religion. The disturbing prevalence of Marxism infiltrating religious teachings reveals rampant moral decay in churches across America. Rather than standing on foundational Biblical principles in the political sphere, many religious leaders avoid taking a stance, fail to vote, or bow to political parties out of family tradition or fear of cultural backlash. This is manifest cowardice. "We see them!" The pathology of the house negro dominates American pulpits, as church leaders, complicit with Leftist Progressive Marxism, have embraced "another gospel" warned about in Galatians 1:8-9. If Malcolm X deemed them "political chumps" and "traitors," how much worse are they in the eyes of God? Pray for religion/Faith institutions in America. A profound truism states, "The condition of America is the report card of the church."

There are countless examples of the archetypes and pathologies Malcolm X observed. When viewed honestly, these archetypes provide an accurate framework for understanding the motivations and behaviors of the entire American electorate. The three pathologies Malcolm X highlighted—the overlord, the house negro, and the field negro—are not only still present today but are also ubiquitous, profoundly shaping the American political landscape. A concise review of these pathologies will help clarify the question: "Which one are you?"

The first is the *Overlord* pathology, characterized by those who wield immense global influence. Overlords are typically billionaires with control over key domains such as media, entertainment, academia, and social institutions. Their motivations often center on the pursuit of global governance and control, employing mechanisms such as depopulation tactics, climate mandates, vaccine mandates, and pandemic dictates. If you have significant global influence, immense wealth, and a desire to control mass populations (totalitarian and authoritarian), you align with the pathology Malcolm X characterizes as an overlord.

The next pathology is the *House Negro Syndrome*. This group consists of those who make decisions based on prevailing cultural and ideological trends. They avoid "rocking the boat" and are quick to conform, even when it contradicts their moral, ethical, or faith-based principles. Those who fall into this category feel comfortable with America's current trajectory, even as it moves toward a "new global order" rooted in Marxist ideals.

They unquestioningly follow mainstream media, cultural trends, or family traditions. Their loyalty can be bought with compensation—whether through money, prestige, or status.

They will diligently support the prevailing orthodoxy, even if it means alienating friends and family who hold different views. These individuals tend to make voting decisions based on personality, race, ethnicity, or charisma rather than demonstrated competence or a proven track record. If you align with this description, you fit the pathology Malcolm X described as a house negro.

The final pathology influencing the American political landscape is the *Field Negro Syndrome.* (Full disclosure: this is the psyche that drives me in all domains of life; I am a proud and unapologetic field negro). This syndrome is characterized by fierce independence and defiance. It is the same spirit that motivated historical figures like Frederick Douglass, Harriet Tubman, and Sojourner Truth to risk their lives for freedom.

This pathology embodies what Margaret Sanger referred to as "the rebellious ones," individuals who could not be bought, sold, or bargained with. It is driven by an insatiable and unstoppable desire to be free of any structure or constraint that infringes upon free speech, free thought, inalienable God-given rights, and human dignity. The field negro is strong, courageous, and cannot be subdued by threats, cancellation, doxxing, public shame, or any other tactics designed to silence them.

In the face of collective groupthink, the field negro refuses to conform or obey, demanding to live free and on their own terms.

I have no doubt that, due to the uncomfortable truth of

these pathologies, many will try to convince themselves that they don't fit into any of these characterizations. However, the reality is that regardless of race, ethnicity, or any other factor, everyone in America falls into one of these archetypes. With so few in America potentially fitting the overlord characterization, the consideration for average Americans is between whether they fit the house negro vs. the field negro characterization. Most people are either motivated or inspired to participate in these three pathologies. But, what about those who may not be driven by motivation, but rather by compulsion or coercion? These are considered cultural conformists. With undo pressure, they conform, and by definition, these fit into the house negro characterization.

Most of us have family and friends who have been swept into one of these pathologies and are fully operating out of them. Depending on their archetype, communication may become difficult, even impossible, and our relationships clouded with frustration and dread. But now, we have a tool to help provide clarity, using the rich history of figures like Douglass, Tubman, and Malcolm X's profound insights. By revealing and illuminating these pathologies, we can help others better understand and make informed choices. In the end, everyone must answer the question: "Which one are you?"

Still not sure? Here's a simple litmus test to finally determine whether house negro or field negro: Anyone who is not motivated to be fiercely independent and demand uncompromising free speech, free thought, free expression, and all other innate freedoms, operates within the pathology of the house negro. In contrast, those who are driven to remain independent and are defiantly committed to freedom (even at great risks) embrace the field negro pathology. *Freedom!*

In the end, *freedom* is the key criterion. The essential question is: "Are you free?" Do you want to remain free? Well, it's time to decide: <u>"Which one are you?"</u>

Acknowledgments

I extend my deepest gratitude to Ms. Regina Roundtree-Wekesa for her exceptional contributions, especially in cover design. Regina's unwavering dedication, marketing insight, and creative intuition have been invaluable to this project. Her tireless efforts and God-given talents in social media and graphic design consistently exceed expectations. I am profoundly grateful for her outstanding work and, most importantly, her cherished friendship.

I also wish to express my sincere appreciation to Dr. Christian Overman, whose insightful critique and constant push for excellence significantly shaped the outcome of this book. His perspectives provided valuable edits and refinements to key issues, and I am grateful for his commitment to truth and his steadfast friendship.

Mr. Richard W. Stevens, in addition to being a valued friend, served as an editor. His edits, profound prose, and intellect are deeply reflected in this project. Richard's depth of understanding of contemporary issues and his editorial prowess helped refine concepts, providing the necessary clarity and momentum for the successful completion of this work.

Numerous friends generously contributed insights and perspectives to this book, but none have been more instrumental than Rodney and Beverly Mayberry. Since the inception of this manuscript, they have been tireless intercessors, encouragers, and supporters, always offering valuable input and profound perspectives to enrich this work. Without their encouragement and support, this book would not have been as impactful.

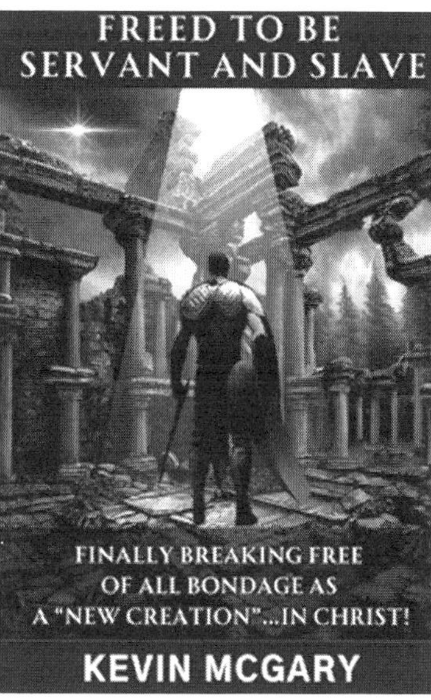

Additional resources:

Every Black Life Matters (EBLM) www.everyblm.com

- Follow us on all Social Media platforms
  - o (YouTube/FB/Insta)
- Racial Unity and DEI Training and Consulting
- Racial Unity and DEI certification

DEI GUY on *Locals* (https://thedeiguy.locals.com/)

Other McGary books **Amazon.com**:

- Freed To be Servant and Slave"DEI In 3D" *Deciphering Designs Demands and dilemmas of DEI*
- "**WOKEd Up!** *Finally Putting an Ax to the Taproot Of White Supremacy and racism in America*"
- "**The War On Women from The Root to The Fruit**… which side are you on?"
- "**Just Justly Justice!**"
- "**Instanity!**"

For Training and Speaking engagements, please contact: kevin@everyblm.com

Made in the USA
Middletown, DE
18 October 2024